Thomas Sankar

OHIO SHORT HISTORIES OF AFRICA

This series of Ohio Short Histories of Africa is meant for those who are looking for a brief but lively introduction to a wide range of topics in African history, politics, and biography, written by some of the leading experts in their fields.

Steve Biko
by Lindy Wilson
ISBN: 978-0-8214-2025-6
e-ISBN: 978-0-8214-4441-2

Spear of the Nation (Umkhonto weSizwe): South Africa's Liberation Army, 1960s–1990s
by Janet Cherry
ISBN: 978-0-8214-2026-3
e-ISBN: 978-0-8214-4443-6

Epidemics: The Story of South Africa's Five Most Lethal Human Diseases
by Howard Phillips
ISBN: 978-0-8214-2028-7
e-ISBN: 978-0-8214-4442-9

South Africa's Struggle for Human Rights
by Saul Dubow
ISBN: 978-0-8214-2027-0
e-ISBN: 978-0-8214-4440-5

San Rock Art
by J.D. Lewis-Williams
ISBN: 978-0-8214-2045-4
e-ISBN: 978-0-8214-4458-0

Ingrid Jonker: Poet under Apartheid
by Louise Viljoen
ISBN: 978-0-8214-2048-5
e-ISBN: 978-0-8214-4460-3

The ANC Youth League
by Clive Glaser
ISBN: 978-0-8214-2044-7
e-ISBN: 978-0-8214-4457-3

Govan Mbeki
by Colin Bundy
ISBN: 978-0-8214-2046-1
e-ISBN: 978-0-8214-4459-7

The Idea of the ANC
by Anthony Butler
ISBN: 978-0-8214-2053-9
e-ISBN: 978-0-8214-4463-4

Emperor Haile Selassie
by Bereket Habte Selassie
ISBN: 978-0-8214-2127-7
e-ISBN: 978-0-8214-4508-2

Thomas Sankara: An African Revolutionary
by Ernest Harsch
ISBN: 978-0-8214-2126-0
e-ISBN: 978-0-8214-4507-5

Patrice Lumumba
by Georges Nzongola-Ntalaja
ISBN: 978-0-8214-2125-3
e-ISBN: 978-0-8214-4506-8

Thomas Sankara

An African Revolutionary

Ernest Harsch

OHIO UNIVERSITY PRESS

ATHENS

Ohio University Press, Athens, Ohio 45701
ohioswallow.com
© 2014 by Ohio University Press
All rights reserved

Printed in the United States of America
Ohio University Press books are printed on acid-free paper ⊗ ™

24 23 22 21 20 19 18 17 16 15 14   5 4 3 2 1

Library of Congress Cataloging-in-Publication Data
Harsch, Ernest, author.
 Thomas Sankara : an African revolutionary / Ernest Harsch.
   pages cm. — (Ohio short histories of Africa)
 Includes bibliographical references and index.
 ISBN 978-0-8214-2126-0 (pb : alk. paper) —
 ISBN 978-0-8214-4507-5 (pdf)
1. Sankara, Thomas. 2. Presidents—Burkina Faso—Biography. 3.
Burkina Faso—Politics and government—1960–1987. I. Title. II.
Series: Ohio short histories of Africa.
 DT555.83.S36H37 2014
 966.25052—dc23
                              2014029649

Cover design by Joey Hi-Fi

Contents

List of Illustrations   7

Preface   9

1. "Another Way of Governing"   13

2. The Forging of a Rebel   20

3. Onto the Political Stage   37

4. The State Reimagined   52

5. Mobilizing the Nation   71

6. Development for the People   88

7. A Foreign Policy of One's Own   108

8. The Last Battles   127

9. "Is It Possible to Forget You?"   146

Selected Bibliography   155

Index   159

Illustrations

Thomas Sankara 16

Sankara during his officer training 25

Sankara serving as a soccer referee 57

Active elders in community mobilizations 75

Members of the Women's Union of Burkina 83

Water reservoir 89

Sankara and a colleague planting a tree seedling 100

Sankara at a conference in Ouagadougou 120

Sankara with President Jerry Rawlings of Ghana 123

Captain Compaoré, Commander Lingani,
    and Captain Zongo 129

Pibaoré villagers rallying in support of the
    Sankara government 145

Preface

Writing this short account of the life of Thomas Sankara required making a number of choices and judgment calls. Given space limitations, which aspects to explore in some detail, which to touch only lightly? Although Sankara was a complex, multisided individual, he was above all a political actor. So the focus here is on his political views and undertakings, especially during his four years as president.

I knew Sankara. I spoke with him directly on half a dozen occasions, a couple times at length. I was also able to observe him giving public addresses and in other interactions while I was covering developments in Burkina Faso as a journalist. This limited familiarity has led me to highlight certain aspects of his personality and style. It may as well introduce some subjective bias. I do not apologize for my sympathies, but simply wish to alert the reader that my interpretations may differ from those of scholars who were less favorable to Sankara's revolutionary outlook. At the same time, I take note of certain shortcomings of his time in office that some of those who idolize him might prefer to pass over.

Sankara clearly played a leading, even preponderant role in his country's revolutionary process, but it was nevertheless a collective enterprise. It had many other actors, both in the leadership and on the ground. Their contributions cannot be given their due attention in a biography such as this, which necessarily focuses on an individual. Nor is it possible to assess Sankara's precise role and influence with full certainty. Some initiatives obviously were his own. Yet his convictions led him to work through collective leadership bodies, making it hard to pinpoint precisely how his views and actions shaped developments. Accounts by some of his contemporaries have helped shed patches of light on these questions. I hope that future scholarship will illuminate yet more.

In my research on this period in the history of Burkina Faso, I am indebted to a number of individuals. Some of those I interviewed are cited in the bibliography. In particular, I would like to thank Paul Sankara for his personal observations about his brother, and Madnodje Mounoubai for sharing several anecdotes about his time working with Sankara. Others living within Burkina Faso or outside the country also provided insights, but I will refrain from thanking them by name.

Among scholars, Bruno Jaffré has conducted the most detailed research into Sankara's life, and his *Biographie de Thomas Sankara* was invaluable in the writing of chapters 2 and 3 in particular. I thank him for reviewing this book's manuscript and making several useful observations. I also appreciate Eloise Linger's sharp editorial eye, as well as the comments and suggestions of the publisher's two anonymous reviewers.

To date, the most comprehensive source for Sankara's own words is the collection published by Pathfinder Press, *Thomas Sankara Speaks: The Burkina Faso Revolution, 1983–87,* available in both English and French editions. The reader interested in more than the short passages from Sankara used in this biography is directed to that collection. I am grateful to the publisher for permission to use its English translations of the quotations drawn from it. For the many quotations taken from other sources, the translations from the original French are my own.

1

"Another Way of Governing"

The women had traveled from across Burkina Faso, packing the tiered seats and spilling into the aisles of the central auditorium of the House of the People in Ouagadougou. There were more than three thousand of them, young and old, a few with babies on their laps, most dressed in multicolored traditional fabrics, often in the red, white, and dark blue pattern of the Women's Union of Burkina. They had come to the capital to celebrate their day—March 8, International Women's Day—with speeches, slogans, stories, songs, and dance. They cheered and chanted with leaders of the women's union, who spoke sometimes in French and sometimes in Mooré, Jula, or Fulfuldé, three of the country's indigenous languages.

That day in 1987 they also came to hear their energetic young president, Thomas Sankara, who had already initiated numerous measures to improve women's standing and opportunities. Sankara's speech did not disappoint. He had made some of the main points before: that women had to organize, that traditional customs had to shed their oppressive features, that social inequality had to be combated, and that the revolution would triumph only if women became full participants. But this time he also anchored his arguments to an exhaustive review of women's oppression through eight millennia of social evolution and gave numerous examples of its signs in contemporary Burkinabè society, sometimes in poetic flights of oratory. He scathingly criticized Burkinabè men—including some among his fellow revolutionaries—who hampered advancement for the women in their own families. Transformation would be incomplete, he said, if "the new kind of woman must live with the old kind of man," drawing much applause and laughter.

Sankara's interaction with the women that day was not unusual. Since becoming president in August 1983 at the head of a revolutionary alliance of young radical military officers and civilian political activists, he had repeatedly traveled across the country to outline his government's ambitious initiatives and projects. On his tours he met with villagers, youth leaders, elders, artisans, farmers, and other citizens. He addressed enthusiastic audiences. Many listeners knew that his words were not just the promises of another politician or government official. They had already seen tangible improvements in their own towns and villages: new schools, health clinics, sports fields, water reservoirs, and irrigation dams. People were impressed by the uncharacteristic vigor of this leader, who was not only impatient to battle poverty but also quick to jail bureaucrats caught stealing from the meager public treasury. Some certainly were alarmed by the revolutionaries' rhetoric about class struggle and calls to crush those who opposed the government. Yet Sankara himself demonstrated a particular ability to convey his sweeping vision of societal transformation in concrete terms and actions that could be readily appreciated by ordinary people and by reformers across ideological boundaries. Until he was cut down in a military coup in October 1987, Sankara was widely seen as having done more to stimulate economic, social, and political progress than any previous leader.

Sankara left a mark beyond his own country. During visits elsewhere in Africa or at international summit meetings, his speeches struck listeners with their forcefulness and clarity. His frank criticisms of the policies of some of the world's most powerful nations were all the more notable coming from a representative of a small, poor, landlocked state that few had previously heard of.

The French authorities had heard of it, at least by the name Haute-Volta (Upper Volta), as they called the territory they had colonized and ruled from 1896 to 1960. When President François Mitterrand visited Ouagadougou in November 1986, he encountered a changed country, with a different kind of leader. President Sankara greeted his guest not with the usual diplomatic niceties and ceremonial toasts. He offered a "duel" of ideas and oratory. Sankara began with a plea for the rights of the Palestinian people; defended Nicaragua, then under attack by

Thomas Sankara (1949–1987). *Credit: Ernest Harsch*

US-backed "contras"; and scolded Paris for its policies in Africa and toward African immigrants in France. Recalling the spirit of the French revolution of 1789, he said his government would be willing to sign a military pact with France if that would bring to Burkina Faso shipments of arms that he could then send onward to liberation forces fighting the apartheid regime in South Africa. If Sankara's verbal jousts took Mitterrand off guard, the French president recovered quickly. He set aside his prepared remarks and took on Sankara point by point. He also praised the Burkinabè president's directness and the seriousness of his questions. With Sankara, Mitterrand said, "it is not easy to sleep peacefully" or to maintain a calm conscience. Half jokingly, he added, "This is a somewhat troublesome man, President Sankara!"

It was not only the Sankara government's daring foreign policy positions that resonated across Africa. People noticed the way he set about governing his own country—with dramatic shake-ups of lethargic state institutions and procedures, prompt trials and prison sentences for wayward officials, and a major shift in public services away from the privileged elites and toward the poorest and most marginalized. Such steps struck many as examples of the kind of deep reforms needed in so many African countries after decades of repressive and corrupt misrule. The rhetoric of Sankara's revolution was not about Western-style representative democracy—for most of Africa, that wave of change was still a few years off, in the 1990s. But it was about reorienting the state back toward the initial promise of the independence era: to overcome the inequalities bequeathed by colonialism, to see to the welfare of the common citizen, and to build a sovereign Africa, free of foreign tutelage.

Radicals and restive youths across the continent were easily drawn to Sankara's example. So were some reform-minded professionals, including Colonel Ahmadou Toumani Touré in neighboring Mali. He later told me that already in the 1980s he was deeply disturbed by the corruption and autocratic methods of Mali's longtime ruler, Moussa Traoré. At the time, he looked to Burkina Faso as a model of "another way of governing, a departure from the form in which a president replaces the colonizer but lives exactly like the colonizer, completely cut off from the living society." (Several years after Sankara's death, Touré led a coup against the Traoré dictatorship and initiated a constitutional process that brought multiparty elections and the restoration of civilian rule. A decade later, Touré, then a retired general, was elected president, although his tenure was not as innovative as many had hoped. As Mali plunged into rebellion and chaos, he too was ousted in a coup in March 2012.)

Improving the ways of governing in Africa has never been easy. As Sankara was to tragically discover in his own country, efforts to restructure state institutions, carry out controversial reforms, and chip away at elite privileges can foster resistance and opposition, both from within and

18

from powerful external forces. Mistakes, brash initiatives, and heavy-handedness can shake the confidence of potential supporters. And seemingly minor differences with close comrades can deepen under pressure. Sankara was killed by some of those comrades on October 15, 1987. That act cut short the life of one of contemporary Africa's more innovative leaders.

However brief Sankara's passage, his life is worth examining. This short account looks at the influences that helped shaped him, the ideas and visions of a self-professed dreamer, and the concrete achievements, ambitious projects, and unfinished work of his presidency. In the process it may help provide some small understanding of why so many youths across the continent continue to see Sankara, decades after his death, as an embodiment of their hopes and dreams.

2

The Forging of a Rebel

Thomas Sankara was born on December 21, 1949, in the small town of Yako in central Upper Volta, as the territory was then called. He too initially bore a different name: Thomas Noël Isidore Ouédraogo. Ouédraogo is one of the most common family names among the Mossi, the largest ethnic group and the mainstay of the old precolonial Mossi empire. Yet Thomas was not Mossi. He was Silmi-Mossi, a socially marginal category descended historically from both Mossi and Peulh. His father, Joseph Sankara, was Silmi-Mossi, but had assumed the name Ouédraogo when he joined the French army in World War II at the request of the Mossi chief of Téma, to whom his family was allied. In the army Joseph also converted to Catholicism from the Islam practiced by most Sankaras. Thomas's mother, Marguerite Kinda, was Mossi by birth and herself had sometimes used the name Ouédraogo. Only later, when Thomas was in his teens, did Joseph change the family name back to Sankara.

Thomas grew up in a large family. Two sisters were born previously, but he was the first son. Eight more brothers and sisters came afterward (and another sister died in infancy). As the oldest boy, Thomas saw it as his duty to help care for and protect his siblings.

His early years were spent in Gaoua, a town in the humid southwest to which his father was transferred as an auxiliary gendarme. As the son of one of the few African functionaries then employed by the colonial state, Thomas enjoyed a relatively privileged position. The family lived in a brick house with the families of other gendarmes at the top of a picturesque hill overlooking the rest of Gaoua. But Thomas played with other children and sat alongside local classmates once he started primary school, so he soon became aware of their conditions and of the wider world around him.

In the 1950s, Upper Volta was still a colony of France. The territory had initially been conquered by French army contingents in 1895–96, when they drove the Mossi emperor (*mogho naba*) from Ouagadougou. It took several more years for them to conquer the Bobo, Samo, Lobi, Gourounsi, Gourmantché, Peulh, Tuareg, and other peoples. Even then, not all communities were "pacified" until the suppression of a major revolt among the peoples of the west and of the northern Sahel in 1915–16. At the time, the territory was part of a larger French West African colony. Only in 1919 was it formally established as a separate colony called Upper Volta. Viewed from Paris, Upper Volta was a minor colonial possession, of little material value except to grow cotton or to provide conscripted young men to work on roads, railways, and plantations in other French colonies. Its marginal status was confirmed when in 1932 the official colony of Upper Volta was dissolved and most of its territory merged into the neighboring Côte d'Ivoire (Ivory Coast), only to be reconstituted yet again in 1947.

Compared with the practice in France's richer colonial territories, Paris sent relatively few French administrators or colonists to Upper Volta. There were enough in Gaoua, however, for the young Thomas to notice how differently they lived from the African population and how much more privileged were the European children of his age. Occasionally he got into scraps with European children in school or around the town. Although his father often took his side in such disputes, he also disciplined him at home for getting into conflicts. When Thomas was eleven years old, just a few days before Upper Volta attained its formal independence from France, he and some friends organized their own mock ceremony to lower the French flag and raise the colors of the new nation. That led to a brawl between European and African boys. Although Thomas himself was not involved, the school director demanded that his father punish him with a beating. His father refused.

Most of the time Thomas applied himself seriously to his schoolwork, excelling in math and French. He went to church often, participated in a church scout troop, and devoted time to religious studies. Impressed with his energy and eagerness to learn, some of the priests encouraged Thomas to go on to seminary school once he had finished his primary courses. He initially agreed. But he also took the exam required for entry to the sixth grade in the secular educational system, and passed. When his father told the priests that Thomas would not be joining a seminary after all, they responded that he had not prayed hard enough for his son.

Thomas's decision to continue his education at a *lycée* (state secondary school) proved to be a turning point. That step got him out of his father's household, since the nearest lycée was in Bobo-Dioulasso, the country's commercial center. He spent hours exploring the large city on a bicycle. At the lycée (named after Ouezzin Coulibaly, a preindependence nationalist), Sankara made some close friends, including Fidèle Toé, years later to be named a minister in his government. Soumane Touré, soon to become another longtime friend, was in a more advanced class, where he participated in a student strike against the school's rather rigid disciplinary rules. Sankara continued to concentrate on his regular studies. He still did well in math and French, took part in theater productions, went to the movies, and started a regimen of physical exercise.

Meanwhile, the country was experiencing political turmoil. Upper Volta's first president, Maurice Yaméogo, was never a particularly inspiring figure, having acceded to independence rather reluctantly. He maintained a strong connection to France, with numerous French "advisers" working in both the army and the civil administration. Over time Yaméogo became more autocratic and jailed many critics. He appointed relatives to key positions and engaged in extravagant personal spending, while simultaneously imposing austerity on state employees and cracking down on the trade unions. He appeared oblivious as his unpopularity grew. On January 3, 1966, workers launched a general strike, and large crowds of students, unemployed youths, workers, petty traders, and others poured into the streets of Ouagadougou in a veritable popular insurrection. After army officers refused to follow the president's orders to disperse the demonstrators by force, it was clear that Yaméogo was finished. He agreed to resign and hand power over to the army commander, Lieutenant Colonel Sangoulé Lamizana.

Those events in the capital stirred few immediate ripples in Bobo-Dioulasso. Sankara was focused on his final secondary school exams. He did hear over the radio, however, that Lamizana had established a new military academy in Ouagadougou, the first in the country, and that as part of its first class of prospective junior officers it would take in three students who had just obtained their secondary school certificates. The military was popular at the time, having just ousted a despised president. It was also seen by some young intellectuals as a potentially national institution that might help discipline the inefficient and corrupt bureaucracy, counterbalance the inordinate influence of traditional chiefs, and generally

Sankara during his officer training in the late 1960s.
Credit: Courtesy Paul Sankara

help modernize the country. Besides, acceptance into the military academy would come with a scholarship; Sankara could not easily afford the costs of further education otherwise. So he took the entrance exam and passed. He joined the academy's first intake of 1966, at the age of seventeen, stepping onto the same career path that his father had once pursued.

As with his earlier studies, Sankara took the challenges of the military academy seriously. Although the physical training was rigorous, especially for someone of modest build, he persisted and strengthened himself. He also discovered that he had an aptitude for leadership—the basic goal of the academy, after all, was to train officers for a new army that had relatively few.

The academy also taught its trainee officers a variety of academic subjects, including in the social sciences. For those topics it employed civilian professors. One was the academic director, Adama Touré, who taught history and geography. Although known for some progressive ideas, Touré did not openly air all his views; that would have been risky in such a politically and socially conservative country. Only years later was it revealed that he belonged to the clandestine African Independence Party (PAI), a regional Marxist group centered in Senegal and with branches in several other former French colonies. Touré invited a few of his brightest and more politically inclined students—Sankara among them—to join informal discussions outside the classroom. Touré talked about imperialism and neocolonialism, socialism and communism, the Soviet and Chinese revolutions, the liberation movements in Africa, and similar topics. Although Sankara had already started to become politically aware, this was the first time he was exposed, in a systematic way, to a revolutionary perspective on Upper Volta and the world.

Besides his official studies at the academy and extracurricular political activities, Sankara also made the time to explore Ouagadougou and widen his network of friends. He pursued his passion for music and played the guitar more often.

Three years later, Sankara completed his studies at the military academy. He was one of just two graduates then selected for more advanced officer training in Antsirabé, in Madagascar, an island nation off the continent's southeastern coast and another former French colony. When Sankara arrived in October 1969 he encountered a country very different from the poor, arid nation he knew. Madagascar was lush with vegetation; its main cities were filled with many historic buildings, monuments, and gardens; and the level of economic development was notably higher.

At the Antsirabé academy, the range of instruction went beyond standard military subjects. Sankara was particularly drawn to courses on agriculture, including how to raise crop yields and better the lives of farmers—themes he would later take up in his own country. Madagascar's army was innovative in another respect: it had not only combat personnel but also members of public service units—the "green berets"—who focused primarily on development activities. Sankara was so impressed that he asked for a year's extension in Madagascar to work with the units.

Beyond widening his knowledge and range of skills, Sankara used his time in Madagascar to improve his mastery of French. He was especially fond of coining words and phrases and engaging in humorous wordplay, which made him a more interesting and effective public speaker. He honed his writing skills, even becoming the editor of the academy newsletter. And he lost no opportunity to supplement his official instruction with further political education. Among the works used in his classes were some by Marxist authors or the well-known French development thinker René Dumont. Several professors were left-wing French academics, and Sankara sometimes had dinner with them.

Sankara advanced his political education through more than books and discussions. He was able to personally witness revolutionary change. His last year in Madagascar coincided with an unprecedented period of political upheaval marked by peasant revolts, general strikes, huge public demonstrations against a conservative pro-French regime, and finally a military takeover that steadily brought ever more radical officers into high positions of power. Sankara and a friend from Mali traveled to the capital in the hopes of meeting Captain Didier Ratsiraka, the most radical of the officers and then foreign minister (later to become president). They did meet, but Ratsiraka was busy and rushed off after a few minutes.

When Sankara finally returned to Upper Volta in October 1973, he was a trained officer ready to command. But his head was also bursting with new notions of how an institution such as the army could be used to promote development—and of the need for wider political and social changes. Now twenty-four and a second lieutenant, Sankara received his first command, to train new recruits in Bobo-Dioulasso.

Sankara moved to that city with his much younger brother and sister, Paul (ten) and Pauline (twelve). Sankara felt that the two had not had enough parental discipline, since his mother was indulgent by nature and his father became less strict with age. "He always used to say we were spoiled," Paul recalled. He and Pauline lived with Thomas in the officers' quarters. They both received considerable attention, in contrast to family life in Ouagadougou, where they were just two of many children. Thomas, Paul remembered, "would always check on our homework, pretty much every day." Although there was a domestic servant to help with chores, "We had to take care of our own clothing, washing, putting things in order. That was it, military discipline." The rigorous upbringing included physical exercise. Paul went running with the soldiers, and liked it. The habits he learned from Thomas stayed with him the rest of his life.

Sankara's approach to the new army recruits under his charge was not too different. He found the established military training programs rather archaic, largely copied from those of the French army in the era of Napoléon Bonaparte. So he adapted them and coupled the military training with civic education, as he had learned in Madagascar. In addition to sports and athletic activities on Sundays, he organized civics classes on Saturday mornings, covering topics such as the rights and duties of citizens and the powers of the legislature, military, and courts. At first the recruits were resentful that some of their free time was taken up by the courses, but eventually they became more interested. According to Bruno Jaffré, one of his biographers, Sankara regarded the recruits' awakened interest in civic affairs as "confirmation of his optimism in human nature and encouragement to engage in other similar actions."

Sankara's experiments in Bobo-Dioulasso had begun to draw attention from others in the military but were cut short, to his regret, when he was transferred to Ouagadougou in March 1974. There he was assigned to the army's engineering corps, where he tapped into the technical skills he had acquired during his last year in Madagascar. Sankara spent much of his time traveling around the country, overseeing the building of roads, houses, and other structures. In the process he discovered that certain army officers and government officials were diverting funds, materials, or food or giving their own relatives lucrative jobs. He openly criticized the dealings of several, including the army quartermaster and the minister of transport—even though the latter was a son of the traditional chief of Téma, to whom Sankara's father owed some allegiance. None of the errant officials were punished, but senior officers did start to wonder about this young upstart.

In December 1974, a brief war broke out between Upper Volta and Mali, growing out of a dispute over a contested region stretching nearly 100 miles along their common border. Sankara was among the many sent to the border. He commanded a small group that staged an ambush and captured some Malian soldiers. The exploit was mentioned in the press, contributing to an image of Sankara as a "war hero." Although that label was sometimes cited when he later became politically prominent, it was not one that Sankara used himself. In fact, he thought the war was senseless, having erupted over some badly drawn lines on a colonial map and pitting against each other two poor African countries with shared cultural and ethnic affinities. The experience of the war also appears to have further alienated Sankara from the military's higher command. It confirmed in his eyes that the officers were more attentive to lining their own pockets than to the conditions of their troops or the need for an efficient, professional army capable of defending the country. It was not hard to see that the army was outmatched by the Malian armed forces, and was saved from defeat only by the intervention of regional mediators who helped arrange a truce in early 1975.

Although Sankara shared his views selectively with some other young officers and with his left-wing civilian friends, he did not express them openly at the time. Yet some of his observations about the weaknesses of the country's army did gain a hearing among his superiors. President Lamizana in particular appreciated Sankara's evident energy and talents. Already at that time, Lamizana recalled years later, he regarded Sankara as an "officer of the future" who was destined to lead. Lamizana was less concerned than some of his colleagues about the unconventional political views circulating within the junior officer corps. Sankara, for his part, treated Lamizana with respect and paid courtesy calls to the general's house on holidays.

In 1976 Lamizana appointed Sankara, now a full lieutenant, to take charge of a new national commando training center. Based in Pô, a relatively small town not far from the southern border with Ghana, the center was designed to train the elite fighting units that the army lacked. For the more than four years he commanded the center, the position provided Sankara with an opportunity to develop more fully the kinds of innovative training programs he had first started in Bobo-Dioulasso—and without having to report daily to any superiors, since he was the highest-ranking officer in Pô. The center's regimen was rigorous, with an emphasis on imparting advanced military skills to the soldiers, who came to Pô from units around the country. Sankara also saw to their well-being.

When he discovered that the military camp lacked a secure source of water, he bought a motorized pump without going through the army's normally slow requisition channels, and then presented the bill directly to Lamizana (who covered it from a presidential account). Noticing that the younger soldiers often spent all their pay early in the month, he ensured that they set up savings accounts at a local bank and learned how to manage their money.

Sankara worked as well to raise the soldiers' civic awareness and intellectual acumen. Yet organizing educational activities was not a simple task. Books were few in Pô, so every time Sankara or his colleagues went to Ouagadougou, they came back with books, some of a political nature. Since the goal was to produce citizen-soldiers who viewed themselves as serving the wider society, Sankara also initiated development projects in which his troops worked directly with local communities. In one instance, the center joined with a nongovernmental organization to dig wells and improve residents' access to water. On another occasion, he secured a contribution of musical instruments, which were given to soldiers with some aptitude to form a band. Sankara, with his guitar, participated in the rehearsals and even some of the performances. As the soldiers got better, they joined with civilian musicians to launch the Missiles Band of Pô, often playing at weekend dances and other events.

In 1978, while Sankara was away for a short training course, there was a physical altercation between some

soldiers and local youths. A superior officer in Ouagadougou sided with the soldiers, worsening the tensions.
Sankara then rushed back to Pô, disciplined the soldiers
involved, and arranged a reconciliation meeting between
the army and the residents.

Since Pô was less than a hundred miles from the capital, Sankara was able to travel there regularly, both to meet
with his army superiors and to see his friends. During
this period, he met a young woman, Mariam Serme. They
began seeing each other regularly, and the romance deepened. They married in Ouagadougou in 1979, in a simple
ceremony in a small Catholic church. Since the couple's
combined income was relatively modest, they originally
planned to invite only a hundred guests to the reception.
But friends contributed generously, and attendance ultimately swelled to three hundred. A little more than two
years later, in August 1981, Sankara became a father with
the birth of his and Mariam's first child, Philippe.

Though focused on his responsibilities at the training center and on his new family life, Sankara remained
painfully aware of the desperate conditions facing his
country's people. In one of the poorest nations in the
world, Upper Volta's 7 million inhabitants had an annual average per capita income of just $210 in 1980. Less
than one in ten lived in a city, and the adult literacy rate
scarcely reached 11 percent. Only 18 percent of school-
age children were in primary school, and a bare 3 percent
made it to secondary school. Recurrent droughts, soil

erosion, and stagnant crop yields meant that hunger was common. Poor nutrition and disease cut lives very short: average life expectancy was an abysmal forty-four years.

Fueled by anger at such a reality, Sankara's conviction deepened that fundamental change must come. During his visits to Ouagadougou, and on yet more military training missions to France and Morocco, he systematically pursued contacts with those who thought likewise. Some were in the military, including Blaise Compaoré, whom Sankara first met during the war with Mali and then again at a training course in Morocco. In 1978 he made Compaoré his deputy commander at the Pô training center. Other contacts were with civilians, members of a number of small, leftist groups. A few groups had followings in the trade unions, but the newer ones were most often based among academics and students. Ideologically, they tended to identify as Marxist, with the supporters of the African Independence Party (PAI) generally politically sympathetic to the Soviet Union and the rest looking to either China or Albania for inspiration. Some groups spent a lot of time debating arcane theoretical points and did not always seem fully aware of the daily problems facing ordinary people.

Although Sankara valued and learned from these activists' debates and discussions, he avoided joining any of the civilian groups. He remained closest to his small circle of friends among the junior officers, and he encouraged interactions between them and the civilian activists, some of whom regularly visited the commando center in Pô.

To Sankara and his colleagues, a scent of change seemed to be in the wind. The politicians of the old conservative political parties were in disarray. Strikes were becoming more common across the country. Public anger was mounting over the recurrent exposure of corruption scandals involving both military officers and civilian bureaucrats. Yet Sankara's study of revolutions had taught him that it could be foolhardy to act precipitously. So he bided his time—at least for a little while longer.

3

Onto the Political Stage

As the 1980s opened, the government of Sangoulé Lamizana had already been in office for nearly a decade and a half. Compared to the experience of some of Upper Volta's more volatile and highly repressive West African neighbors, Lamizana's rule was relatively stable and not especially strict. Yet his government's relative laxity came with a corollary: there was very little effort to tackle the country's severe social and economic problems. Development initiatives were minimal at best, while those in high office—with the apparent exception of the president himself—freely used their positions to advance their own personal interests and aggrandizement. As Lamizana complained in a 1980 New Year's address, the elites cared little for the good of the country and instead worshipped "the religion of power and money."

For many other military officers of Lamizana's generation, this was not particularly troubling. What did concern them was the government's inability to end the incessant bickering of leading civilian politicians or rein in the restive student and labor movements, which were becoming more active.

On November 25, 1980, a group of senior officers led by Colonel Saye Zerbo mounted a coup. Adopting the rather unwieldy name of the Military Committee for the Enhancement of National Progress (CMRPN), they deposed the government, detained Lamizana and other officials, scrapped the constitution, dissolved the National Assembly, and suspended all political parties and activities. Zerbo, a veteran of French military campaigns in Indochina, cited an "erosion of state authority" under Lamizana among the reasons for his coup. He vowed to instill discipline within the state and fight corruption, and to that end set up commissions to study civil service reform and investigate malpractices by officials of the previous regime. The coup was initially popular. The new government set up by the CMRPN included some progressive nationalist civilian ministers and enjoyed the support of some trade unions.

Sankara took no part in that coup. Even though some young officers rallied to the CMRPN and Sankara and his closest friends were sympathetic to the new regime's promises to root out corruption, they remained suspicious of the political conservatism of the colonels now in power. Their position was a delicate one. On the one hand, as members of a military hierarchy, they were obliged to follow their superiors. On the other, they hesitated to accept public positions in the new government out of concern that to do so might compromise their strategic goal of fundamental political change. The reality was that the radical wing of junior officers represented by Sankara was not yet strong enough to decisively influence events.

Nevertheless, the radicals' support was growing among the ranks of the military, just as their ties were deepening with the student and labor movements and with the civilian revolutionary groups. For the officers of the CMRPN—whose early popularity soon began to wane—this support was a political asset that could shore up their hold on power. They embarked on a game of seduction to draw in the young radicals.

As an acknowledgment of Sankara's military command abilities as well as his political following, he was promoted to captain in January 1981 and named head of the army's operational division. He soon was asked to take on a ministerial position in the government. Sankara refused. In a carefully worded letter to Zerbo, he cited "a personal, free, and conscious decision to not accept any political post." Some of his civilian revolutionary friends agreed with that decision. Others urged Sankara to take up the offer, arguing that outright rejection could expose him and his comrades to retaliation. Finally, after some negotiation, Sankara reluctantly agreed to become minister of information. He insisted, however, on two conditions: that his deputy at the commando training center in Pô, Blaise Compaoré, take over as its commander; and that Sankara serve as minister for only two months until a replacement could be found (although his tenure ultimately stretched to seven months).

On September 13, 1981, Sankara assumed his first official political position. Even though he viewed his new duties as temporary, he set about fulfilling them with the same seriousness and attention to detail as he devoted to other tasks. He brought in a trusted friend from his secondary school days, Fidèle Toé, to act as his chief of staff and recruited several promising young journalists to help him oversee the work of the state-owned media.

From the outset, Sankara functioned like no other government minister up to that time. With a flair for the dramatic gesture, he pedaled to work each day on a bicycle rather than drive a state-issued car. The sight of a cabinet minister bouncing along Ouagadougou's dusty streets just like other citizens sent a clear message of the kind of public servant he intended to be.

To journalists, Sankara's approach to the work of the Ministry of Information was very different from that of his predecessors. He did not urge them to mince their words or paint official life in glowing colors, but instead quietly encouraged them to report what they saw. Years of state intimidation were not easy to shake off—and some reporters may well have been suspicious of this new minister in uniform. But gradually the general tenor of the official media became more probing. Exposés of high-level scandals now appeared not only in *L'Observateur,* a private newspaper, but also in the state-owned weekly *Carrefour africain.* Articles revealed massive embezzlement at a publicly owned investment bank by its former head and raised questions about an official in the Ministry of Trade who was suspected of taking bribes in exchange for authorizing illegal wheat imports.

The revelations stirred public outrage, but the only trials at the time were of several corrupt post office personnel. Predictably, conservative state officials were not happy with the exposés. Security police called in the director of the national news agency for questioning, accusing him of publicly leaking details of the investment bank scandal. Sankara reacted immediately by protesting directly to the minister of the interior. In a follow-up letter he argued that such acts could divert the press from its basic mission: to provide citizens with "the most accurate information possible."

Meanwhile, political and social tensions in the country were again sharpening. While the CMRPN's promises to clamp down on corruption and profiteering proved to be of limited substance, its reaction to political dissenters took on a much harder edge. Outspoken student activists were detained. As labor unions continued to demand better living and working conditions, the authorities responded by suspending the right to strike; dissolving the most militant of the union federations; and ordering the arrest of its central leaders, including Soumane Touré, one of Sankara's secondary school friends. Touré was reported to have evaded arrest by fleeing to Pô in the automobile of Ernest Nongma Ouédraogo, Sankara's cousin. The CMRPN's ever more repressive and antilabor turn prompted Sankara and other radical junior officers to step up their own political activities, through "circles of reflection" within the military and in discussions of strategy with their colleagues in the student and union movements.

Sankara also decided that the time had come to end his participation in the government. Since the CMRPN had ignored his earlier requests to be relieved of his functions, Sankara finally took the initiative himself. He made his exit in a particularly theatrical and politically charged fashion. On April 12, 1982, just three days before the officers of the CMRPN were to hold the first major review of their time in office, Sankara sent a formal letter of resignation to the president. In it he criticized the CMRPN for its "class" character and for serving the "interests of a minority." He also announced his resignation publicly—and live over the radio—during a speech at the closing session of a conference of African ministers responsible for cinema. With President Zerbo present at the event, he issued a strong plea for freedom of expression, concluding with the words: "Woe to those who would gag their people."

The senior officers reacted promptly by arresting Sankara. They also demoted him in rank and deported him to a military camp in the western town of Dédougou.

Sankara's open defiance reflected a broader split between the conservatives and the radical junior officers. It widened further during the review assembly three days after Sankara's exit, leading to the resignations from the CMRPN of Compaoré and Henri Zongo, another captain close to Sankara. They too were exiled to remote military bases.

Although communication among the core leaders of the radical officers' wing was now more difficult, they were able to remain in sporadic contact, while others took a more direct role in keeping the network active. They were emboldened by the CMRPN's increasing political isolation. Some of Zerbo's rivals within the factionalized army raised the idea of another coup, and quietly approached the radicals to join the anti-Zerbo plotters. In discussions with his colleagues, Sankara rejected that option, arguing that a strictly military takeover would not be able to initiate fundamental political and social change. Instead, he maintained, it was necessary to first elaborate a political platform in conjunction with the civilian movements and revolutionary groups.

Though Sankara's supporters held back, other officers moved ahead to military action, led principally by Commander Gabriel Somé Yorian, the army chief of staff. On November 7, 1982, they overthrew Zerbo's CMRPN and proclaimed a new military-led government, which they called the Council for the Welfare of the People (CSP). The new body was a coalition of individuals and factions united only by opposition to the Zerbo regime. It initially had no agreed political platform and no established leadership, enabling the radicals to push it in a somewhat progressive direction. Their influence was evident in the CSP's first declarations, which condemned the Zerbo regime for waste, corruption, illicit enrichment, and repression of students and workers. They also won agreement to restructure the CSP as a wide consultative body of 120 representatives from all military units in the country.

Sankara himself happened to be in Ouagadougou at the time of the coup, having received permission to visit his family after the birth of his second son, Auguste, just a few weeks earlier. His presence in the capital fueled inaccurate rumors that he had been a key force behind the coup. Given the leadership vacuum in the CSP, some of his supporters did in fact put forward his name for the presidency, which he declined. Others nominated Somé Yorian, but the radicals blocked that choice since the commander was known as a political conservative who was close to Maurice Yaméogo, the country's first president. Ultimately, Jean-Baptiste Ouédraogo, the little-known head of the army's medical service, was the compromise choice as president.

Although the revolutionary-minded junior officers were just one component of the broad coalition in the new CSP, they exerted greater influence than ever before. Two close Sankara allies, Commander Jean-Baptiste Lingani and Second Lieutenant Hien Kilimité, became secretary-general and deputy secretary-general, respectively, of the CSP. One of the body's first acts was to restore Sankara, Compaoré, and Zongo to their previous ranks as captain.

As he did when he was minister of information, Sankara used this new opening as a public platform to agitate for more change. Although he was not yet a member of the government, the CSP sent him to speak on its behalf in late December to a congress of the secondary and

44

university teachers' union, one of the most militant in the country. Telling the teachers that the army was facing "the same contradictions as the Voltaic people," Sankara affirmed that "struggles for liberty" were gaining within the military barracks and vowed that the new government would support union rights. A commentary in the independent newspaper *L'Observateur* noted that while fiery pronouncements were routine for trade union leaders, this was "the first time an officer of the Voltaic armed forces had made such engaged statements in public."

The following month, on January 10, 1983, an extraordinary assembly of the CSP acknowledged Sankara's growing political standing by naming him prime minister. This time he readily accepted. He thus became the official number two to President Ouédraogo and, more importantly, was in charge of coordinating the day-to-day work of the various ministries.

When Sankara took his formal oath of office on February 1, he vowed that he and other government members were there to serve the people, "not to serve themselves." And by "the people," he specifically meant peasants, workers, artisans, artists, students, and democratic organizations that defended the interests of the "popular masses." The people wanted freedom, he said, but "this freedom should not be confused with the freedom of a few to exploit the rest through illicit profits, speculation, embezzlement, or theft." He urged state personnel to get out of their air-conditioned offices, experience the concrete living and working conditions of ordinary citizens, and set a practical example of "probity, honesty, and love of work well-done."

As prime minister, Sankara had his first opportunity to represent his country on the world stage. In late February, much to the unease of France, other Western powers, and some neighbors such as Côte d'Ivoire, Sankara paid an official state visit to Libya. He was greeted there with considerable fanfare and promises from Muammar al-Qaddafi to send substantial aid. That visit (along with a brief stopover in Upper Volta by Qaddafi that April) provided some grist for claims from sections of the media and from Sankara's political opponents that he was a lackey of the mercurial Libyan leader. Qaddafi did indeed press Sankara to adopt his idiosyncratic political theories, but Sankara was reported to have replied: "We are not exactly political virgins. Your experience interests us, but we want to live our own."

Sankara also represented Upper Volta at a summit meeting of the developing countries' Non-Aligned Movement in New Delhi the second week of March. There he actively sought out various revolutionary leaders, including Fidel Castro of Cuba, Samora Machel of Mozambique, and Maurice Bishop of Grenada. In his speech to the summit, Sankara openly sided with the more radical wing of the Non-Aligned Movement, including by supporting anti-imperialist rebels in El Salvador and the revolutionary Sandinista government in Nicaragua.

Within Upper Volta, Sankara also became more overt in expressing his revolutionary views. On March 26, 1983, the CSP organized a mass rally in Ouagadougou featuring its top officials. Commander Lingani, as secretary-general of the CSP, gave a short introduction, vowing opposition to "exploiters" and "imperialist subversion attempts." Sankara, as prime minister, took the podium next. He strenuously defended his foreign policy initiatives, including his overtures to various revolutionary leaders around the world. But most pointedly, he also took sharp swings at virtually all sectors of Upper Volta's social and political elites: bureaucrats, businessmen, party politicians, religious and traditional leaders, corrupt officers. He spiced up his characterizations of these "enemies of the people" with a lively litany of colorful animal imagery, such as "fence-sitting chameleons" and "hungry jackals." Throughout the speech, he employed a call-and-response method to elicit the crowd's vocal participation:

Are you in favor of keeping corrupt civil servants in our administration?

[*Shouts of "No!"*]

So we must get rid of them. We will get rid of them.

Are you in favor of keeping corrupt soldiers in our army?

[*Shouts of "No!"*]

So we must get rid of them. We will get rid of them.

When Sankara finished, President Ouédraogo stepped to the podium to read his own speech. But he had been clearly upstaged by his prime minister. His own address was delivered in a markedly lower key and had a more moderate message.

Some weeks later, on May 14, another rally was organized in Bobo-Dioulasso. A similar scenario played out. Sankara elicited a very enthusiastic response from the members of the youth organizations invited to the rally. When President Ouédraogo stood up next to address them, he was greeted at first with silence. Then as he spoke the crowd began to disperse, amid chants of "Sankara! Sankara!"

Sankara's various pronouncements, at home and abroad, cemented his alliance with the country's main revolutionary political groups. But they also alarmed the more conservative officers in the CSP—and apparently the French authorities as well. Two days after the Bobo-Dioulasso meeting, Guy Penne, the African affairs adviser to President François Mitterrand, arrived in the country for an official visit. Early the next morning, May 17, armored units surrounded Sankara's home and took him into custody. Others took up strategic positions around the capital and arrested Lingani. Although surrounded, Captain Zongo rallied a number of troops and vowed to resist, but relented after speaking by phone with Sankara, who urged him to avert a bloodbath. His friend and political activist Valère Somé managed to evade arrest and traveled to Pô, where he alerted the commandos about the coup. In the absence of Captain Compaoré (who was traveling), the commandos mobilized and took control of the town. When Compaoré joined them, they decided to openly refuse to recognize the legitimacy of the authorities in Ouagadougou.

The new government—widely known as the CSP-II—still had Jean-Baptiste Ouédraogo as its titular president, but Somé Yorian was now the real power behind the regime. With Sankara out of the way, Ouédraogo met later that day with Penne, who promised generous financial aid from France.

If Sankara's ouster was supposed to restore political stability, it soon became obvious that the move was backfiring. Protests erupted almost immediately. Over May 20–21, large and sometimes violent demonstrations rocked Ouagadougou, involving high school students, youths from poor neighborhoods, and some trade unionists. Protesters cried, "Free Sankara!" and chanted anti-imperialist slogans, particularly against France, widely regarded as the promoter of the coup.

The demonstrations, together with the defiance of the commando base in Pô, prompted the authorities to relent somewhat. Sankara and Lingani were freed for a while in an effort to start negotiations. Sankara was even permitted to travel to Pô, where he was greeted as a hero. Sankara, Lingani, and Zongo were soon rearrested, however.

As a political stalemate seemed to set in for the next two months, the "Sankarist" camp gradually consolidated its position. Sensing that a new regime change was imminent, political discussions between the young officers and civilian groups advanced to the point of sketching out a general political platform and deciding who would be named to key ministerial posts. Meanwhile, clandestine committees of civilian supporters were formed, drawn from the leftist groups, student movement, and trade unions. Messengers shuttled back and forth between the oppositionists in Ouagadougou and the commandos in Pô, where some students and other youths underwent military training. Meanwhile, Sankara continued to negotiate with President Ouédraogo in the hopes of arranging a peaceful political transition and avoiding bloodshed. At a meeting with Sankara on August 4, Ouédraogo reportedly indicated his willingness to resign as president.

According to some accounts, Captain Compaoré's forces in Pô obtained information that Somé Yorian was preparing a decisive initiative of his own: to assassinate Sankara, Lingani, and Zongo; push President Ouédraogo aside; and assume power in his own name. That prompted the rebels to strike first. On the afternoon of August 4, 1983, commandos from Pô headed for the capital, leaving the Pô garrison under the guard of armed civilians. The commandos traveled quickly in trucks commandeered from a Canadian construction firm, slipped into the capital, and took up positions around key locations: the presidency, radio station, security and gendarme headquarters, and the armored group at Camp

Guillaume. The clandestine civilian groups played a central supporting role, as guides and by cutting the city's power. At 9:30 p.m., in a closely coordinated operation, the commandos seized all their main targets, as junior officers led takeovers at the air base and the artillery camp. They confronted only minimal resistance, and as a result very little blood was shed. (However, Somé Yorian and another conservative officer, Fidèle Guébré, were captured several days later and shot, supposedly during an "escape attempt.")

By 10:00 p.m. on August 4 Sankara was on the radio to announce the overthrow of the government and the start of a new revolutionary process. In a declaration broadcast several times during the night in French, Mooré, and Gourounsi, he proclaimed the creation of the National Council of the Revolution and called on citizens throughout the country to form popular committees to safeguard it. The new government's main goal, he said, was to defend the people's interests and to help them achieve their "profound aspirations for liberty, true independence, and economic and social progress."

4

The State Reimagined

When Sankara and his colleagues took power on August 4, 1983, they called their leading body the National Council of the Revolution (CNR). The name signaled to anyone who might have been in doubt that their goal was sweeping political and social change. The next day, Ouagadougou witnessed a huge welcoming demonstration, the first of many support marches and rallies over the following weeks and months in towns and villages across the country. The response in the streets indicated that major sectors of the public—especially young people—had high expectations that finally something would be done to fundamentally refashion their country.

Sankara, then just thirty-three, did not waste time. He soon outlined the broad sweep of his revolutionary vision: an overhauled state to serve the interests of all citizens; the elimination of ignorance, illness, and exploitation; and the development of a more productive economy to reduce hunger and improve living conditions.

While the CNR would be in the lead in spurring such changes, Sankara insisted that ordinary people also had to organize and take initiative. In response to his first radio broadcast as president appealing to everyone, "man or woman, young or old," to form popular organizations, new Committees for the Defense of the Revolution (CDRs) began to emerge within a few days. The first arose in a rather disorganized manner in Ouagadougou's poorer neighborhoods and then spread more systematically over the next few months to other towns and most of the approximately seven thousand rural villages.

Throughout his presidency, Sankara spoke and acted in the name of two institutions, the government and the CNR. The government, which implemented policy, comprised both military and civilian ministers, the latter chosen because they represented the main left-wing parties or because of their particular technical or managerial skills. The CNR, also a body of soldiers and civilians, deliberated periodically on broad policy matters and guided the work of the government. The CNR's precise membership was kept secret for security reasons, although it was widely known that Sankara, Compaoré, Zongo, Lingani, and Valère Somé were among those belonging to it. Decision making in the CNR was collective—and on some occasions proposals favored by Sankara were overruled. But Sankara clearly was the CNR's most influential member, and his energy, acumen, and oratorical skills ensured that he would be its most visible public face.

Revolutionary Vision

Sankara delivered the CNR's main programmatic declaration, known as the "political orientation speech," in October, two months after the takeover. It included a broad critique of the established order as well as an ambitious agenda for transformation. There was little difference between colonial rule and "neocolonial society," Sankara said, except that some nationals had taken over as the agents of foreign domination. While the twenty-three years of Upper Volta's independence was "a paradise for the wealthy minority, for the majority—the people—it is a barely tolerable hell." Echoing the themes of his "enemies of the people" speeches in May, Sankara identified the main domestic opponents of revolutionary change as the "parasitic classes" and the traditional "reactionary forces" in the countryside. In contrast, the main proponents were the "people," principally workers, the petty bourgeoisie, and peasants.

The character of the revolution, he said, was "democratic and popular." Its long-term goal was "to eliminate imperialist domination and exploitation and to purge the countryside of all the social, economic, and cultural obstacles that keep it in a backward state." In place of the old state machinery, a new one would be built that would be "capable of guaranteeing the democratic exercise of power by the people and for the people," with the CDRs as the main agents of that process.

Sankara's use of the term "democratic," it should be noted, drew from notions of participatory democracy, not Western-style electoral models. In fact, one of the CNR's first measures was to outlaw the country's established political parties, which were seen as tools of the old elites. No elections to representative parliamentary bodies were envisaged. The absence of elections—except within the framework of the obviously partisan CDRs—was later seen as one of the Sankara government's major shortcomings, even by most of those who continued to follow his ideas. Despite the rhetoric of people's participation, there were insufficient channels through which popular ideas and grievances could be transmitted upward.

Throughout Sankara's October 1983 address and in other speeches, the influence of Marxist ideas was evident. Sankara readily acknowledged his appreciation of the Russian, Chinese, and Cuban revolutions. During visits to his office it was easy to spot volumes by Marx and Engels on his bookshelves and a bust of Lenin on his desk. Sankara read widely, including the Bible and Koran and writings by many non-Marxist revolutionaries and other progressive thinkers. Whatever his personal views, Sankara was careful to not tag the labels of "socialism" or "communism" onto the revolutionary process he was helping to lead. Upper Volta, he pointed out, was an extremely underdeveloped country, with little industry and just a tiny wage-earning working class. Under the circumstances, the process there was "an anti-imperialist revolution" that was unfolding "within the limits of a bourgeois economic and social order." The most important tasks facing revolutionaries were therefore to fight against external domination, construct a unified nation, build up the economy's productive capacities, and address the population's most pressing social problems, such as widespread illiteracy, hunger, and disease.

To symbolize that rebirth, the CNR changed the country's name in August 1984, during the first anniversary of its assumption of power. The territory once labeled Upper Volta would henceforth be called "Burkina Faso," translated roughly (from two different indigenous languages) as "land of the upright people." Besides emphasizing integrity and probity as essential characteristics of the new state, the name also signaled its indigenous identity, with its citizens—now known as Burkinabè—projected to be proud Africans.

Leadership Style

Whatever people thought of Sankara's grand ideas for the country, they soon became aware that his day-to-day conduct was markedly different from that of any previous president. At times with theatrical symbolism, he openly disdained the customary pomp and ceremony that generally come with high office. Official portraits of the president—so common in public buildings across Africa—were prohibited. Young activists were discouraged from chanting his name. He was normally driven to meetings and public events not in limousines, but in modest cars. Once a week he played soccer with his advisers and staff, and passersby could see him dressed in shorts and jersey. Sometimes he appeared unannounced at public events, participants only gradually becoming aware of his presence when they glanced to the side or

Sankara serving as a soccer referee. His presidential style was very informal. *Credit: Courtesy Paul Sankara*

rear and saw him quietly standing there, perhaps wearing a tracksuit.

Such informality was designed to send a message: that leaders should be modest, and that especially in such a poor country, they should not live the high life. In 1987, Sankara's last year, he publicly declared all the sources of income and assets of himself and his wife, Mariam. They were quite modest: he clearly had not used his position to amass wealth. His two sons remained enrolled in public school. Mariam continued to report daily for her job at the government's shipping agency, where she was a transportation specialist. His parents lived in the same house they occupied before in Ouagadougou's Paspanga neighborhood, his father now retired but his mother still selling spices and condiments to bring in some extra income.

Paul, his younger brother, said that Sankara told all family members that they should not anticipate any benefits because of his political position, in contrast to the common practice in much of Africa. "He explained to everybody how we shouldn't expect anything from him." He also warned them to "be careful of people coming with gifts," since they would likely seek some favor in return. Sankara noted in an interview with a Burkinabè journalist: "I've taught those close to me that they should in no way try to profit from the fact that one of their relatives now happens to be president. Whatever they may earn, let them earn it because they've worked for it, not because they're members of the president's family, neither my wife, nor my brothers and sisters, nor my other relatives or my children when they grow up a bit more."

Sankara did name a few personal friends to high positions, as well as a cousin, Ernest Nongma Ouédraogo, as interior minister. All had been politically active for years. Sankara trusted their loyalty, as well as their willingness to tell him what they thought, rather than what they thought he wanted to hear. "Friendship was important to him," recalled Paul. His brother believed that "real friends tell me exactly what they want to tell me, even if I don't like it."

Alfred Sawadogo, who worked with Sankara as an adviser on nongovernmental organizations from 1984 until the coup, has described a complex, multisided individual: "He was always surprising: Sometimes exuberant, quarrelsome, teasing, funny, friendly, and warm. Sometimes hard, withdrawn, quick-tempered, stony faced. Sometimes lyrical and poetic, his words powerful, deep, and real. But always true to himself: a nationalist to his core, an idealist, demanding, rigorous, an organizer."

Sankara could be stubborn in his views, even when they were unpopular. Yet he could also reverse himself when persuaded that he was wrong. In a draft of a speech that he was to have given to a group of military comrades on the day of his death, Sankara noted that "we have benefited each time that someone considered it necessary to raise an opinion different from mine, to defend a position different than mine. . . . These I have adopted and implemented, along with advice, suggestions, and recommendations."

Sankara was always eager to learn new things, including new technologies. At a time when personal computers were still rare in Africa, he and his cabinet ministers took courses in how to use them. He also began to learn English.

Sankara's methods of work were unconventional. Although trained at military academies in rigorous planning and strategic thinking, he sometimes took initiatives in an ad hoc fashion, with little evident forethought about how they could be implemented. "Sankara was the antithesis of a bureaucrat," Sawadogo commented. Sankara hated formalism and cumbersome, slow procedures. Functioning alongside the president, Sawadogo learned to "work fast, think fast, act fast, make decisions and be fully responsible for them." Sankara did not like it when anyone told him that a particular initiative had never been tried before or was impossible to carry out. He frequently declared, "That which man can imagine, he can achieve." Over time, Sawadogo recalled, those who worked with the president learned that by aiming for the seemingly unattainable, they were able to accomplish much more than they had ever dreamed—they could push the boundaries of what was possible.

Ordinary Burkinabè seemed to readily embrace Sankara's approach, as they mobilized in their local communities to quickly build new schools, health clinics, and other facilities that had once seemed but a remote fantasy. But many of the country's civil servants were less eager to step up the pace. Sankara discovered that he had to combine persuasion with a good bit of coercion to get them to move more quickly and effectively in responding to people's needs.

Disciplining the Bureaucracy

An early priority was to convince state employees—and the population at large—that the CNR was serious when it said that public property was sacred and that civil servants were there to serve the public, not themselves. Up until then, the record had been otherwise. During the first two decades of the country's independence, only about thirty cases of economic crime were brought before the courts, and very few of those involved high-level perpetrators.

That changed dramatically with the creation of the People's Revolutionary Tribunals (TPRs). Their purpose was both repressive and educational, to punish crimes of corruption and embezzlement, and to instill a greater sense of morality in public life. Ernest Nongma Ouédraogo, interior minister under Sankara, later explained to me that the aim of the TPRs was "to awaken people, to put them on guard against corruption, and to prevent those who might be tempted by corruption to pull back." Sankara made a similar point in his speech at the opening of the first TPR trial, declaring, "To the immoral 'morality' of the exploiting, corrupt minority, we counterpose the revolutionary morality of an entire people acting in the interests of social justice."

Ordinary citizens, moreover, were to help implement that justice. Departing from the practice of the old courts, in which a single magistrate ruled over a case, the new tribunals were established as panels of professionals and lay judges, including one magistrate, perhaps a military or police officer, and five or six civilians chosen by local CDRs. The trials were public, often drawing large audiences and with the proceedings broadcast live over the radio. Cassette tapes recorded from the trial broadcasts sold briskly in marketplaces.

The first trial, in January 1984, was of General Lamizana, who was charged with diverting money from a special presidential fund. After hearing extensive testimony that Lamizana had used the fund mainly to help a variety of individuals, not for his own personal enrichment, the panel decided by majority vote to acquit him. Not everyone was so fortunate. A dozen more TPR trials over the next six months included among their defendants forty-four former government officials of cabinet rank or above. A dozen were acquitted, but the rest were ordered to pay stiff fines and reimburse money they had embezzled. A number also received jail sentences, with Colonel Saye Zerbo drawing an eight-year term for embezzlement, illicit enrichment, and tax fraud. Overall, about forty tribunal sessions were held under the CNR, most of them taking up multiple cases, with nearly one thousand individuals tried.

For other government functionaries who might be tempted to improperly benefit from their positions, the message was clear: henceforth, state office was to be regarded as a public trust, with public goods and affairs managed on behalf of the population, not in the officeholder's own interests.

Not all disciplinary measures led to trials. To help shake up a bureaucracy that moved at a lethargic pace, a number of civil servants were simply fired for incompetence, spending working hours in bars, or being politically disloyal.

In a country where civil service salaries were far above the incomes of most other Burkinabè and the public sector took up a big share of the state budget (leaving little for public services or investment), Sankara's CNR also tightened up considerably on the incomes and perks that state employees had come to expect. Numerous bonuses were simply eliminated. Various "solidarity" funds were set up to aid drought victims or contribute to public investment campaigns, with the contributions deducted directly from government employees' pay packets. These measures caused considerable disgruntlement throughout the civil service, even though the higher echelons generally had to give up a bigger share.

Government ministers and other senior officials lost their expense accounts. Two-thirds of the government's auto fleet was sold off, and only small cars were kept, even for ministers. Officials who were assigned individual cars were strictly prohibited from keeping them outside working hours without permission (to prevent them from using the vehicles for informal business activities).

In August 1985, with no prior warning, the CNR dissolved the government. It relieved all cabinet ministers of their titles and reassigned them to collective farming projects in the countryside. Most were subsequently reappointed. A similar government dissolution/reconstitution occurred each of the following two Augusts. Sankara explained that this was a "revolutionary pedagogic formula," designed to destroy the "myth" that ministerial appointment was an irrevocable sinecure for the individual holding the office. "Everyone must know that a minister is only a servant, and that each militant must be prepared to take on governmental duty."

An Army of the People?

Like other state institutions, the military itself was marked for change. Sometimes the political rhetoric became overheated, as leaders of the CNR stressed the need to "decolonize" the army and transform it from an instrument of the bourgeoisie into a servant of the oppressed. Sankara, in line with his earlier work in the army, often emphasized the importance of raising the political and civic consciousness of the ranks, stating that "a soldier without training is just a criminal in power."

Yet the process of reforming Burkina Faso's armed forces was rather more orderly and measured than the verbiage might have suggested. The military chain of command continued to operate normally—except that its very pinnacle was essentially lopped off, both by the death or imprisonment of those senior officers who had opposed Sankara's radical wing and by the compulsory retirement of all the army's remaining generals. Since no other officers were promoted to that rank, the Burkinabè army remained devoid of generals until many years later.

Like other parts of the state administration, the military too had suffered from corruption and profiteering under the old regimes. To clean house, the CNR hauled a number of senior officers before the TPRs, and some were found guilty and imprisoned. New "revolutionary discipline" councils were set up within the armed forces to hear cases of embezzlement, theft, unauthorized absence from duty, and other infractions. New "garrison committees" were also established, along the lines of the civilian CDRs, with representatives elected by general assemblies of officers and ranks. The instructional program at the commando training base in Pô was expanded for the first time to include basic officer training, so that trainee officers no longer had to be sent abroad for their initial studies.

Most significantly, Sankara's earlier experiment in linking military training with public service and development work was made systematic. Military bases around the country started farms to grow food and raise livestock, engaged in tree planting to combat deforestation, cleaned up trash from towns and villages, dug wells, and built schools, health clinics, roads, and other facilities. Aside from its practical impact, this kind of activity had an educational function: to help prevent soldiers from developing superior attitudes and to convince civilians that the army, alongside its usual functions, could also contribute to the country's economic advancement.

By farming, Sankara told me in 1984, soldiers would be further reminded of how ordinary Burkinabè labor and suffer, so that they would continue seeing themselves as part of the people, not members of a privileged group. "This is the way we are going to produce a new mentality in the army." At the same time, he added, military training was being extended to civilian supporters through the CDRs and establishment of a reserve militia, in effect serving to "demystify the military arts." Henceforth the defense system would be composed not only of the army. "It is composed of all the people. This is possible because the people trust us. In how many African countries do you see them giving arms to civilians?"

Yet the reality was not quite so rosy. Arming young and inexperienced CDR activists led to abuses. And some of the underlying weaknesses of the regular army were highlighted during another brief border war with Mali in late December 1985. The Malian government attacked, using the presence of Burkinabè census takers in a disputed region as a justification. The Burkinabè armed forces, with only a small air force and very few tanks or armored cars, were no match for the larger and better-equipped Malian military. The Burkinabè side suffered serious setbacks. Fortunately, mediators negotiated a ceasefire five days later, and both countries agreed to submit their border dispute to arbitration by the International Court of Justice.

Some armed CDR and militia units had joined the army in trying to defend the country during the war, but the sobering reality was that popular mobilization could not compensate for the military's fundamental shortcomings. Sankara acknowledged that the CNR had neglected equipping the army, believing that it would have been "criminal to spend money on arms." Throughout his presidency, total regular troop strength remained steady at nine thousand men. Military expenditures, as a share of total spending, hovered around 19 percent, only slightly higher than when the CNR first took over.

Decentralization

The new state envisaged by the CNR was not only one intended to be less corrupt and more effective, but also one that extended—practically for the first time—outside the main cities and towns. Previous regimes had tried to govern the countryside only indirectly, largely through traditional chiefs and other local notables. They saw little need for building up an administrative apparatus outside Ouagadougou and a few other centers. But if the Sankara government was to extend public services to the rural population and initiate reforms to break the hold of the chiefs, then it needed to extend the state's limited geographical reach considerably.

The CDRs played a major role in this. Although their main functions were to help mobilize local communities for development projects and to support the CNR politically, they also had a quasi-state role. Sankara referred to them as "representatives of revolutionary power in the villages, the urban neighborhoods, and the workplaces."

The CDRs' fundamental decision-making body was the general assembly, a regular meeting of all members to discuss pressing questions and make decisions by majority vote. The assemblies elected nine-member CDR bureaus to direct activities and liaise with higher-level CDR bodies. The local CDR units were genuinely popular and not just for the educated few, filled with people from humble social origins, many of them illiterate and unable to speak languages other than their own.

The CDRs had to undertake a wide range of local responsibilities, from ensuring the provision of basic social services and day-to-day security to helping out with the national census and publicizing government directives. In much of the countryside, CDRs were the main centers of political power, especially given the "insufficiency of official services," as one CDR report put it. For all practical purposes, the CDRs were the basic building blocks for a restructured state apparatus.

The CDRs played their roles in direct competition with the traditional chiefs. This was the first time in the country's postcolonial history that institutions other than the chieftaincy or councils of elders existed in the villages, representing at least the beginnings of a shift in authority to commoners. The central government itself stepped in to weaken the position of the chiefs. Although the chiefs' prerogatives had been challenged before, Sankara went further. In December 1983 he decreed the abolition of all laws on the designation of chiefs and their territorial jurisdictions and stripped them of any remaining state benefits or rights to collect taxes, tributes, or labor services.

A month earlier, the CNR started a process of creating new territorial divisions and local government structures. Thirty provinces were created, significantly smaller in size than the old regions to ensure better administrative coverage of their populations. Below the provinces were three hundred new departments, an average of ten per province. And below them were the villages and urban communes. Each department was managed by a council selected by the village and town CDRs within that department, but headed by a prefect directly appointed by the central government. The thirty urban communes that served as provincial capitals were run by government-appointed "special delegations," with mayors chosen by the CDRs (except in Ouagadougou, where the mayor was a government appointee).

In trying to extend its authority down to the local level, the government faced numerous challenges, not least of which was its limited personnel. Since it did not have money to simply recruit additional civil servants to staff the new provincial structures, it opted to partially decentralize some of the functions and personnel of the central ministries, setting a quota for each relevant ministry to shift an additional 10 percent of its employees to the provinces.

In the past, most ordinary Burkinabè had scarcely any contact with state representatives. Now, for better or worse, the state was starting to become a much more active presence in their daily lives.

5

Mobilizing the Nation

On an especially hot day in March 1987, during a visit I made to Doundouni, about 40 miles west of Ouagadougou, some 50 residents crowded into the village's only primary school classroom. They were especially proud of the new facilities they had built themselves: a health post, an entertainment hall, a nearby cereal bank, and a headquarters for the local Committee for the Defense of the Revolution (CDR). "This is a great day to do things, to involve the whole population," commented one villager. Observed another: "Before, people didn't know how to work together. But now they've learned to work together equally. That's why things are changing in this country."

Scenes like the one in Doundouni were common across the country. In big urban neighborhoods and small villages alike, people mobilized collectively to build new infrastructure, clean up their locales, and tackle many other day-to-day problems. Burkinabè had long been known for their spirit of self-help, hard work, and collective engagement, but to many residents and foreign observers the intensity and pace of community mobilizations clearly had picked up.

"The popular masses are going faster than the government in this matter," Sankara said a day before my Doundouni visit. "When we ask a province to build four schools, they end up building twelve. This causes problems, since we have to provide the seats, tables, chalk, schoolmaster, and so on. Perhaps it's better like this—that the people are zealous, that they're committed and enthusiastic—than if they pull back." While the popular clamor for more education may present the government with some "painfully joyful" difficulties, he added, it was preferable to the situation in some neighboring countries, where the authorities were "sorrowfully lucky" to not have people placing so many demands on them.

Within just a few weeks of the takeover by the National Council of the Revolution (CNR) in August 1983, the collective labor mobilizations began. The initial calls came from the central authorities in Ouagadougou, and at the local level were often initiated by the defense committees. Although social and political compulsion sometimes played a role, the initiatives generally drew a ready and sometimes exceptionally enthusiastic response. Most of the specific goals were of obvious and immediate benefit to the communities: cleaning school and hospital courtyards; graveling roads; building mini-dams to capture or channel scarce water for farm irrigation; and, when building materials could be secured, even starting construction on schools, community centers, theaters, and other facilities. There was also some consultation in the selection, with proposals often raised or discussed during public CDR assemblies.

Bigger projects required more elaborate organization. In the town of Kaya, neighborhood and workplace CDRs spent a week simply gathering the necessary materials to begin construction on a new residential zone. Some days were devoted to locating and transporting large stones or sand. Civil servants and members of the CDR women's units gathered gravel. And different neighborhoods were organized into daily shifts to produce bricks.

In the villages the mobilizations were scheduled to not conflict with normal farming or market activities. In the cities, where the rhythm of life was set more by the standard workweek of salaried employees, neighborhood general assemblies and work mobilizations usually took place on weekends. The pace initially seemed quite hectic. Over the weekend of November 12–13, 1983, alone, seventy-seven separate CDR activities were reported in major towns, nearly half of them being either collective labor mobilizations or other forms of development work.

These community mobilizations were put on a more systematic basis in the People's Development Program (PPD), launched in October 1984. Through the program the government and CDRs tried to coordinate local efforts more systematically on a national scale, extend them into provinces where they had previously been weak, and integrate them better into the government's more general economic, social, and political undertakings. Over the fifteen months of the PPD, 351 schools, 314 maternal health centers and dispensaries, and 88 pharmacies were built, as were 274 water reservoirs and 2,294 wells and boreholes. Across the thirty provinces, people's actual contributions of money and labor (expressed as a rough monetary equivalent) were estimated to have averaged 27 percent of the total costs of the provincial programs, with the remainder funded by the provincial and national governments and by external donor agencies. According to Planning Minister Youssouf Ouédraogo, the PPD was regarded by the government as "a popular school for the masses" to bring them new technical and organizational skills, "so that they themselves can solve the problems that come up in the provinces."

Young people were the most eager participants in the mobilizations, as they were in CDR activities more generally. Sometimes urban youths went to rural areas, as when the CDR in Somgandé, on Ouagadougou's northern periphery, mobilized to help farmers in nearby villages. Noted the weekly magazine *Carrefour africain,* the initiative helped the urban youths appreciate the hard work of village life, while at the same time making villagers more open to "the innovative ideas of the youths."

In the traditional social structures of Burkina Faso, as elsewhere in Africa, elders usually held the greatest social status and often monopolized decision making. But with the arrival of the CNR—many of whose members were themselves relatively young—urban and rural youths finally saw new avenues to break from old social

Youth were most active in community mobilizations, but efforts were also made to draw in elders. *Credit: Ernest Harsch*

constraints. By actively supporting their communities, they not only acquired new organizational skills but also enhanced their own sense of social worth.

Social mobilizations were not a monopoly of the CDRs alone. Across the country, new self-help organizations proliferated, many without any direct connection to the government. Between 1983 and 1987 more than 160 new civil associations were formed, while the membership of an established group such as the "naam" peasants' movement in Yatenga province increased nearly thirtyfold.

Commando Campaigns

Beyond the local level, the CNR launched a variety of "commando" mobilization campaigns to tackle problems of national importance. Participants generally included volunteers, CDR activists, and civil servants reassigned from their normal duties for a few days or weeks at a time. One campaign focused on digging irrigation canals in the Sourou River valley to support agricultural cooperative projects. Another organized people to plant millions of trees to help combat deforestation and the spread of desert areas.

The Battle of the Rail, launched in February 1985, had an especially high profile. Its goal was to extend deeper into the isolated northeast the sole railway line, which then ran from the Côte d'Ivoire border only as far as Ouagadougou. Although the northeast had unexploited manganese deposits, the World Bank and other donor agencies considered extension of the railway to be uneconomical, and therefore declined to fund it. The Sankara government hoped to change their minds by building an additional 100 kilometers of track from Ouagadougou to Kaya through its own financing and labor mobilizations. Within seven months, about a third of the distance was covered, with some four hundred laborers mobilized each day, usually on a rotating basis from different CDRs, government offices, civil associations, and volunteers (including some foreign visitors). By October 1987, when the government was overthrown, track had been laid to within just a few kilometers of Kaya.

Not all commando mobilizations were so productive. In 1985 Sankara proclaimed a "white city" campaign to mobilize townspeople to paint their houses white, as part of a broader effort to improve urban appearances. Many residents strongly resented the effort, however. They objected to the cost of the paint, but mostly they thought the choice of color was ridiculous: with winds blowing around the fine ocher sand of the Sahel, not much stayed white for very long. The campaign was soon abandoned.

The Alpha Commando literacy campaign was better received. Launched in February 1986 and lasting two and a half months, it mobilized mainly volunteer instructors—students, CDR activists, civil servants, and some teachers. They taught basic literacy and numeracy to some thirty thousand rural people, mostly members of peasant associations. With follow-up, about half eventually managed to acquire a measure of functional literacy.

By most estimates, the greatest triumph was the Vaccination Commando, a child immunization campaign. Previous vaccination campaigns were carried out strictly through the government's regular and very limited health services—and thus reached only a tiny fraction of children, even in Ouagadougou. Reflecting Sankara's typical impatience with slow, bureaucratic procedures, the cabinet decided in September 1984 to launch a commando-style campaign to vaccinate most Burkinabè children against the key childhood killers (measles, meningitis, and yellow fever)—and to do so over a period of only two weeks, just two months later. Foreign donor agencies advised against such a fast and extensive campaign and suggested a more cautious, measured approach. The UN Children's Fund

(UNICEF) and a few other donors agreed to support the effort, although with serious misgivings about its feasibility.

According to Paul Harrison, in his 1987 book *The Greening of Africa*, what the international agencies failed to take into account was the government's commitment and ability to mobilize very large numbers of people: "There were radio programmes and posters in local languages; there were travelling theatre groups. But in a country with poor roads, where only a minority have radios, person-to-person communication was central." The CDRs, he noted, were crucial in creating awareness and mobilizing people. "The response was overwhelming. Mothers almost took the vaccination points by assault. They walked long distances, and formed queues often more than a kilometre long, waiting whole days and nights for their turn."

By the end of the two weeks, some 2 million children had received a vaccination, about three times the number in previous campaigns. Rural coverage was almost as high as in the cities. According to a joint evaluation by UNICEF and the Ministry of Health, sensitization of the population to health issues was "the most spectacular aspect of the operation." In addition, health worker morale increased significantly, as did greater overall public demand for better health services. Most immediately, the Vaccination Commando meant that in 1985 the usual epidemics of measles and meningitis—which often claimed the lives of between 18,000 and 50,000 children—did not occur.

Women's Advancement

Even more than male youths, Burkinabè women previously had very few opportunities to mobilize in defense of their social and economic interests, organize politically, or engage directly with state institutions. The weight of traditional, patriarchal relations bore down on them especially heavily. Most women were effectively relegated to the status of minors, whatever their age. From birth to death, many basic life decisions remained in the hands of their fathers, husbands, uncles, and other male relatives. As Sankara observed, "Our society—still too primitively agrarian, patriarchal, and polygamous—turns the woman into an object of exploitation for her labor power and of consumption for her biological reproductive capacity."

From the start, the new Burkinabè leadership emphasized that the emancipation of women was one of its central goals. In Sankara's 1983 political orientation speech, it featured second in a list of national priorities, after reform of the national army but before a section devoted to economic reconstruction. Repeatedly, speeches by Sankara and other leaders chastised "corrupt" and "feudal" husbands for treating their wives and daughters as "beasts of burden" and pledged to act against the many customary practices judged to be oppressive to women.

Specific measures for women were built into many social and economic programs, from literacy classes specially targeted toward women, to the establishment of primary health units in each village, to support for women's cooperatives and market associations. A new family code was drafted. Among other things, it sought to set a minimum age for marriage, establish divorce by mutual consent, recognize a widow's right to inherit, and suppress the bride-price and the practice whereby a widow had to marry one of her late husband's brothers. Vigorous public campaigns were launched against female genital mutilation, forced marriage, and polygamy.

Such practices were deeply rooted in Burkinabè society, however. They could not be eliminated by simple government decree or moral arguments. That did not stop Sankara and his colleagues from trying, but many of their efforts met with widespread rejection and incomprehension—including from some women themselves.

In the political realm, however, the government did have the power to take unilateral initiatives. At a time when hardly any women had reached high political or administrative positions in Africa, Sankara named several to cabinet posts, including as ministers of family affairs, culture, health, and the budget. In each of the last two cabinets under Sankara, in 1986 and 1987, the number of women reached five, or about a fifth of the total; previous governments had, at best, one or two women ministers. Other women were appointed as judges, department prefects, provincial high commissioners, and directors of state enterprises (the national airline, television network, and foreign trade agency).

Women appointees, though highly capable, were not always welcomed. In the province of Passoré, where Aïcha Traoré was named high commissioner, merchants strenuously resisted her efforts to rebuild the central marketplace in Yako. Supporters of the old conservative parties tried to use the presence of a woman in such a high office to rally men against the government.

Yet many women appreciated finally seeing someone of their own sex in at least a few positions of authority. Though more of a gesture than a genuine shift in power between the genders, such appointments sent a strong signal of encouragement to women at all levels.

Some women also received military training—a particularly radical notion in such a society. In some cases, as at the Pô commando base, the training began with the wives of soldiers, partly to enable them to play stronger leadership roles in the defense committees and other organizations. But more formal training programs were also established for women around the country, most of them members of the CDRs. Some women were recruited directly into the armed forces, with a few rising to become tank drivers and air force pilots.

The annual celebrations of International Women's Day, held in both Ouagadougou and the provinces, became high-profile events and provided women with occasions to speak out on issues of immediate concern. Provincial women's assemblies were also held, as in Bam, where women raised problems like female circumcision, forced marriage, inequitable divorce practices, poor sex education, and the banishment of young women who became pregnant outside of marriage.

The most numerous openings for women to organize came through the CDRs. Initially, women took part in the defense committees to only a limited extent, even though they often participated in greater numbers than men in the local community clean-up and development mobilizations. During the very first defense committee elections, almost no women were elected to the local CDR bureaus, in part because few were bold enough to step forward as candidates. In an effort to overcome this gap, the official statutes of the CDRs, issued in May 1984, mandated that at least two positions in each nine-member bureau had to be filled by women, that of deputy chairperson and the executive member responsible for women's mobilization. In some rare cases, more than two women actually were elected.

To help coordinate the work of female CDR activists nationally, a special body was created within the CDR national secretariat, the Directorate for Women's Mobilization and Organization. It sought to direct the women's cells within the CDRs and to encourage women's participation in general assemblies, community development projects, and militia training, although with uneven success. By the second national conference of the CDRs in 1986, one-third of the elected delegates were women.

Members of the Women's Union of Burkina. Sankara stressed the importance of women's political advancement. *Credit: Ernest Harsch*

In September 1985 the Women's Union of Burkina (UFB) was set up by directive of the CDRs' national secretariat. Local UFB bureaus were elected by general assemblies of women, but the chairperson, initially, was the CDR bureau member responsible for women's mobilization. Although it was not independent and UFB members sometimes found themselves relegated to stereotypical female roles such as preparing meals for conferences, the women's union gradually acquired a more distinct profile. During the 1986 literacy drive, for example, a UFB representative sat on each five-member regional management committee. The UFB complained that only limited places had been allotted to women; of the nearly 1,000 literacy centers, just 69 were exclusively for women and 396 for both sexes. These complaints prompted Sankara to promise that future literacy drives would be organized so that more women could take part.

A Nation for All

Like many other African countries, the territory known as Upper Volta/Burkina Faso was something of an artificial creation. The French conquest brought into one entity peoples who spoke some sixty different languages; observed Islam, Christianity, or indigenous African religions; and followed widely varied practices and customs. True, because of the reach of the old Mossi empire, the country's geographical boundaries were perhaps less arbitrary than those of some of its neighbors. And the relatively easygoing relations among the various ethnic groups meant that tensions among them were historically not that severe, despite some resentment over the tendency of the Mossi to dominate. At the same time, the French decision to divide Upper Volta among Côte d'Ivoire, Mali, and Niger between 1932 and 1947; the absence of a strong nationalist movement for independent statehood; and the pervasive influence of French administrators for years after independence tended to impede the development of a robust national identity. Moreover, the sheer weakness of the state and its extremely minimal contact with people in the countryside meant that there was not much of an institutional framework within which a sense of common citizenship could arise.

When Sankara's CNR came to power, it consciously pursued a policy of inclusion, to open up social and political life to more of the country's different ethnic groups. The CNR itself had numerous Mossi in it, but also Bobo, Gourounsi, Peulh, and others. Sankara, who was Silmi-Mossi (of mixed Mossi and Peulh ancestry), personified that mixed composition.

In rejecting the territory's former name, Upper Volta, in favor of Burkina Faso, the government sought to project a new national identity: First, an identity that would be local and African, against the French designation of "Haute-Volta." Second, a pan-territorial identity that encompassed the country's multiple cultures. Roughly translated as "Land of the Upright People," the name Burkina Faso is itself a multilingual composite: *burkina* from Mooré, the language of the Mossi, meaning "worthy people" or "men of dignity"; and *faso* from Jula, signifying, among other definitions, "house" or "republic." The "bè" suffix in Burkinabè came from Fulfuldé, the language of the Peulh.

Even during the year before the name change in August 1984, the state media started to actively promote Burkina Faso's multiplicity of indigenous cultures and languages. Television news was no longer delivered only in French, but also in Mooré and occasionally other languages. Because very few Burkinabè had access to television, radio remained the main means of communication, and it employed eleven of Burkina's indigenous languages. At the anticorruption trials held before the People's Revolutionary Tribunals (TPRs), a radio translator would often sit in a corner with a microphone, to provide a running summary of the proceedings in Jula or one of the other national languages for broadcast.

During the colonial era, all school instruction had been in French, and only later were Mooré, Jula, and Fulfuldé introduced in some primary schools on an experimental basis. Because of the neglect, by the 1980s, only thirty-six of the approximately sixty languages had been studied in any depth, and of those, just fourteen had been given a written form. The Sankara government drafted a new educational reform proposal that projected a greater use, over time, of the national languages in the schools. Although that reform was not implemented, the literacy campaign of 1986 was conducted in nine indigenous languages, despite the scarcity of written materials in them.

The government also supported numerous cultural festivals, at which participants from around the country could share their varied forms of artistic expression. At a weeklong national cultural festival in Gaoua in December 1984, for example, dance troupes, musicians, weavers, sculptors, writers, and painters from different ethnic groups displayed their talents and competed for jury prizes. Among the novelists, poets, playwrights, and short-story writers, there were winners for works in French, Mooré, Jula, and Fulfuldé. Such displays were not confined to occasional festivals. Major political rallies, professional conferences, and other events also were frequently preceded or followed by dance and musical performances by troupes from different ethnic groups.

The Sankara era saw an unprecedented blossoming of African cultural and ethnic representations. Many Burkinabè acquired a strong sense of pride in their specifically African identity and in the cultural richness of their country. Years after the CNR's demise, significant sectors of the population, including leading figures who once were politically hostile to the Sankara government, seem to readily accept their identification as citizens of Burkina Faso, as Burkinabè.

6

Development for the People

Sankara's vision of Burkina Faso's economic transformation was a basic one: improve the lives of its people. When the US magazine *Newsweek* asked him how a poor country like his could develop, he did not lay out a sweeping agenda of industrialization or land redistribution, as the interviewer might have expected from someone who spoke of revolution. Sankara talked instead about building irrigation dams to help grow more food, constructing schools and health clinics, and setting up networks of small stores throughout the countryside so that villagers could secure their daily necessities. "Our economic ambition," Sankara explained, "is to use the strength of the people of Burkina Faso to provide, for all, two meals a day and drinking water."

Most people in richer countries might take for granted access to safe drinking water and more than one meal a day. But in Burkina Faso that was indeed a revolutionary notion.

When I visited the northeastern region of Yatenga, on the edge of the Sahara Desert, it was obvious just how painstaking and incremental economic and social development would be. Even on the outskirts of Ouahigouya, the regional capital, the ground was hard and sunbaked, covered here and there by patches of sandy soil that could support little more than a few shriveled stubs of grain. Only an infrequent jagged tree or parched brown bush dotted the landscape. Yet Traoré, a local farmer, had been able to harvest a modest crop of millet and sorghum a few months earlier. He showed off the rows of rocks that he and his two brothers had piled up along the contours of the land to slow soil erosion and retain crop debris, a new technique he had just learned to marginally

A water reservoir built through community mobilizations. For such a poor, arid country, expanding access to water was a revolutionary measure. *Credit: Ernest Harsch*

improve fertility. Not far from Traoré's farm there were some new wells, a few hand pumps, and numerous small dams and channels to capture and direct water on the rare occasions when it did rain. A few miles farther away the scenery turned unexpectedly green. Farmers tended gardens of carrots, okra, cabbage, and other vegetables. A nearby water reservoir built a couple years before provided the irrigation.

The government's emphasis on such small, tangible improvements did not mean it lacked a grand vision. In Sankara's 1983 political orientation speech, he declared that the aim was nothing less than the construction of a national economy that was "independent, self-sufficient, and planned at the service of a democratic and popular society." That goal was echoed in the first five-year economic development plan, launched in 1986. The slogan of "self-sufficiency," as generally used by Sankara and other leaders, did not mean cutting Burkina Faso's national economy off from the rest of the world. But it did imply reorienting it more toward domestic markets and interests.

Easy to proclaim, excruciatingly difficult to accomplish. Since much of the economy was dominated by family agriculture, with little industry of any kind, there were few sources of domestic revenue to finance expansion of productive capacities or social services.

Yet the National Council of the Revolution (CNR) did set out on a path of gradual transformation. Throughout its various programs, projects, and initiatives, several recurrent themes stood out. First, economic projects had to use local materials, labor, and financing as much as possible in order to reduce reliance on foreign aid and imports. Second, with equity as a watchword, those at the top had to lose some of their perks so that those at the bottom could benefit. Third, whatever limited financial resources the government had at its disposal were allocated as a priority to rural areas, not the urban centers. And fourth, in a country of scant rainfall and a harsh climate, environmental concerns had to be integrated into all development efforts. Previous governments had espoused some of these aims, but none had ever put much effort into trying to implement them.

"We Have to Depend on Ourselves"

At a time when many African leaders behaved like supplicants eager to do anything to attract Western financing, the Burkinabè government insisted that national priorities came first. As the five-year plan put it, Burkina Faso's development strategy had to "base itself on national resources, both human and material, to build the new society."

If Western donor agencies were willing to help finance those national programs, fine. However, Foreign Minister Basile Guissou told me, "we don't wait for anything from anyone. No one will come to develop Burkina Faso in place of its own people." Planning Minister Youssouf Ouédraogo put it in similar terms: "Foreign aid, technical aid, will only be as a support, no longer the determining factor in the construction of the national economy."

They were both echoing Sankara. "We could use and we need aid from developed nations," the president told *Newsweek,* "but such aid is not so generous or forthcoming in these times." Aid from the United States, he noted, was "ridiculously small, especially when you see the wealth and prosperity of that country." Despite the CNR's revolutionary rhetoric, most of Burkina Faso's donors maintained their aid programs. However, much of that aid was tied to specific projects, over which the donors continued to exercise considerable decision-making authority, in contrast to funds allocated directly to the central budget, which the government controlled. France, the largest donor, halted all general budgetary support after 1983. The World Bank did the same after January 1985.

One reason for the Burkinabè authorities' reticence about foreign aid was their concern that it often came with strings attached. Justin Damo Barro, who was finance minister during Sankara's first year, later revealed that he had tried on four occasions to persuade the president to ask for assistance from the International Monetary Fund, but Sankara declined on the grounds that IMF "conditionality" would spell the end of the revolution, by shifting decisions over basic economic policy away from Burkinabè and toward an external entity. During a discussion with me in March 1987, Sankara said that he had earlier asked the US government to stop financing contingents of Peace

Corps volunteers and instead provide an equivalent sum as direct budget support. The United States refused, so the Burkinabè government suspended the Peace Corps program. Even when foreign volunteers carried out useful projects, Sankara said, they might end up fostering "a psychology of dependence on outside aid." As he put it in the *Newsweek* interview, "In the final analysis, we know we have to depend on ourselves."

Austerity of a Different Kind

Since the government's own treasury was not very large, the budget ministry consistently sought to reduce unnecessary and ostentatious spending. This was reflected in the early measures to cut the perks of ministers and other high civil servants. "We have tightened the belt from the top," Sankara remarked. On several occasions, the authorities even organized public discussions of the annual budget, to promote greater understanding of the budgetary process and to solicit more ideas about where to cut. Sankara closed one such conference by inviting citizens to find further ways to economize. He criticized civil servants and state enterprise personnel who still engaged in absenteeism, self-enrichment, laziness, and wasteful working methods. The CNR also strengthened the other side of the ledger sheet by enhancing the collection of taxes (levied mainly on property owners) and other sources of revenue. Meanwhile, it abolished the regressive colonial-era "head tax," a modest amount that every citizen had to pay annually, but which was onerous for poor villagers who had little cash income.

The combination of budgetary rigor and enhanced tax collection—along with foreign aid when it was available on acceptable terms—enabled the government to significantly increase investments, especially in basic infrastructure (roads, wells, market facilities) and essential social services. Between 1983 and 1987 the annual budget increased notably. Expressed as a percentage of gross domestic product, government expenditures rose from 13.4 percent to 17.4 percent and revenue from 13.5 percent to 16.3 percent. On the expenditure side, social services were strongly favored. From 1983 to 1987 public spending on education increased by 26.5 percent per person and on health by 42.3 percent.

Across Africa at the time, "austerity" was a very unpopular word. It generally was introduced at the insistence of the IMF and World Bank, as part of their "structural adjustment programs." The cuts often came in government jobs, education, and health, while the elites were usually able to continue pursuing their profligate ways. In Sankara's Burkina Faso, by contrast, it was the poor who saw the tangible benefits of austerity and those at the top who had to make do with less.

Into the Fields

Burkina Faso is an overwhelmingly agrarian country. In the 1980s more than 90 percent of its population still lived and labored on the land. Farmers had little to work with. In the entire country, less than 6 percent of the land that could be irrigated actually was. The remainder depended almost entirely on rainfall, which was often inadequate and unreliable. Only 10 percent of all farmers used animals for plowing. Most had nothing more advanced than the *daba,* a short-handled hoe. Few livestock herders had access to fodder, and usually roamed the countryside in search of grazing land and watering spots.

In some areas of central and western Burkina Faso, commercial farmers grew cotton, a crop first introduced by force in the colonial era. Since cotton exports still secured nearly half the country's foreign earnings, most official agricultural extension services, fertilizers, and other assistance went to those cotton zones, not to food farmers. As a result, cereal production stagnated. In 1984 the same amount of millet and sorghum—the main staple grains of rural Burkinabè—was grown as in 1960, although the country's population was 50 percent larger. So hunger remained prevalent across much of the countryside, even in "normal" times. In years of drought, many villagers were seriously threatened by famine.

For Sankara, the choice was obvious. Agriculture would be "the nerve and principal lever of our economic and social development," he said in a speech to tens of thousands during a celebration of the government's first anniversary. Most investments would be devoted to agriculture, "especially in favor of food crops." To modernize the country, he said, it would be essential to raise farm yields, put under cultivation all land that could be developed, and reorganize existing agricultural production channels.

In the regular annual budgets, a greater share of spending was shifted directly to agriculture. In the five-year plan, some 71 percent of projected investments for the productive sectors were allocated to agriculture, livestock, fishing, wildlife, and forests. An even larger amount in recurrent spending was planned for irrigation, sanitation, and other water projects, with major portions of health, education, and transport investments destined for rural areas.

Total cereal production rose by a spectacular 75 percent between 1983 and 1986. Much of that increase was due to more favorable rains, and output declined somewhat in 1987 because of poor weather. Yet the improvement in yields was also due to 25 percent more land being placed under irrigation between 1984 and 1987. In the Sourou Valley a dam was built within a few months almost entirely by volunteer labor, with about 8,000 hectares of irrigated land devoted to cereals, rice, and market gardening and another 8,000 to growing sugarcane for a new sugar refinery. Across the country, use of fertilizer increased by 56 percent between 1984 and 1987. Because of the high costs of imported chemical fertilizer, much of this increase involved greater use of organic fertilizers. In 1987, some 180 tractors were imported for a number of large-scale cooperative projects.

To help farmers better store and market their crops, hundreds of village cereal banks were built through collective labor mobilizations organized by the Committees for the Defense of the Revolution (CDRs) and other rural organizations. In the past, villagers, with no way to store any surplus grains, often had no option but to sell them to local merchants (since the state grain marketing agency had the capacity to buy up only about a tenth of the country's crop). The merchants sometimes hoarded cereals to drive up prices, then later resold the grains back to the same villagers at perhaps twice the original cost. But the cereal banks, now managed by farmers groups, allowed villagers to buy back grain when they needed it at only a little more than the initial price (as long as not too much cereal had spoiled in the rudimentary local granaries).

In August 1984 the government enacted a new agrarian reform law, which, among other things, nationalized all land. Previously, most rural land had been owned communally, with the chiefs generally deciding who could farm it. In some areas, however, private land ownership had begun to develop, as urban land speculators sometimes acquired titles, either illegally from village chiefs or from commercial farmers who failed and had to sell their land. For most villagers, the agrarian reform's shift from communal to state ownership would not bring any real change in their relationship to the land; their rights to farm the land remained the same. Yet by ending the risk that farmers could lose land to creditors or speculators, the law aimed to bring farmers greater security of tenure. Sankara emphasized that point at a large rally in the agricultural town of Diébougou the year after the law was adopted. "Improve your land and farm it in peace," he told the residents. "The time is over when people, sitting in their parlors, can buy and resell land on speculation."

The agrarian law also was designed to change how decisions about land were made. In theory, traditional chiefs' powers of land allocation were to be handed over to new commissions run by the village CDRs. That shift could not be put into practice, however. There were very few land-use maps and it was the chiefs who had detailed knowledge about established tenure patterns and rights. Despite the advent of the CDRs, many chiefs still enjoyed considerable authority among ordinary villagers. So when plans for new land management commissions were finally drafted in 1987, they provided for involving local chiefs. However, with the overthrow of the Sankara government later that year, implementation of the new land law ground to a halt.

"Struggle for a Green Burkina"

One other aspect of the agrarian reform, Sankara noted in an October 1985 speech on food security, was to encourage Burkinabè to become more responsible for managing land in a rational way and for preserving the environment more generally. "One cannot imagine the development of agriculture and an increase in its productivity without a program for the regeneration and conservation of nature," he said.

In Africa at the time, the close interrelationship between environmental sustainability and economic development was not yet widely understood by decision makers. Some African leaders were even suspicious of calls for environmental protection, seeing it as a diversion from efforts to industrialize and diversify their economies. The idea that environmental conservation and economic development were complementary gained wider acceptability among African leaders only after they took part in the United Nations' groundbreaking "Earth Summit" in 1992 in Rio de Janeiro, Brazil. In appreciating the importance of the natural environment—"the struggle for a green Burkina," as he put it—Sankara was well ahead of most of his African counterparts.

To many of Sankara's fellow citizens, however, the point was more than obvious. The daily reality of their harsh environment constantly drove the issue home: scarce and fickle rainfall, water holes and rivers that often ran dry, vegetation that became increasingly sparse in the savannah regions, and a sandy, windswept desert that each year seemed to edge farther and farther south from Burkina Faso's northern provinces. Even residents of the capital, Ouagadougou, became acutely aware of the problem one day in March 1985 when the fine red sands of the Sahara Desert blew in on the harmattan winds, blocking the sun, filling the air, and covering everything with a thin coating of grit. "Every one of us understood that the desert is advancing," Sankara remarked a few weeks later, "that the desert is already at our doors."

As early as the 1970s, when Sankara traveled around the country to implement community development and civil engineering projects for the army, he recognized how vital water sources and trees were to ordinary Burkinabè. After becoming president, one of his first acts was to create a Ministry of Water, the first time the country had a ministry devoted exclusively to that essential resource. His government's People's Development Program of

Sankara and a colleague planting a tree seedling. His government was an early proponent of environmental conservation.
Credit: Courtesy Paul Sankara

1984–85 featured many community projects to dig wells and water reservoirs, and included mobilizations to plant more than 10 million trees.

To help raise public awareness and combat the alarming loss of vegetation, Sankara launched a campaign in early 1985 known as the "three struggles." One "struggle" sought to end the unregulated and abusive cutting of trees for firewood, a problem worsened by unlicensed wood merchants who oversaw the wholesale razing of woodlands. Henceforth, Sankara decreed, merchants would have to be licensed to cut only from designated areas and could transport wood only in specially marked vehicles, with violators subject to criminal charges. Another struggle penalized the practice of setting brush fires to clear farmland, an activity that easily escaped control in the dry season. Finally, livestock herders were discouraged from allowing their cattle to wander unsupervised into farming areas where they could trample crops. Sankara warned bluntly that "any grazing animal that destroys a planted tree or cultivated grain will be shot, pure and simple."

The first two aspects of the campaign had only mixed results. While the trade in firewood did undergo some greater regulation, poor villagers continued to cut trees for firewood in the absence of alternative energy sources. And for farmers without heavy tools or equipment, setting brush fires was still often the quickest way to clear land. In face of such prevalent practices, the government and the CDRs simply lacked the capacity to effectively enforce the new prohibitions. Worse, the struggle to halt animals' destruction of trees and crops turned into an unmitigated disaster. Some CDR activists took to extremes Sankara's call to shoot roaming animals. Many were shot, whether they were trampling vegetation or not, and ended up on spits for CDR feasts. A few herders who resisted the practice were also killed, and many fled with their herds, some into neighboring countries. Since farmers and herders often hail from different ethnic groups (many herders are seminomadic Peulh), ethnic tensions also flared. Recognizing that the effort to control wandering livestock was an utter failure, the first national conference of the CDRs in early 1986 decided to abandon it.

According to Alfred Sawadogo, who worked with Sankara to draft the "three struggles" campaign, this experience convinced the president to search for more peaceful, systematic ways to preserve Burkina Faso's environment. The accent shifted from criminalizing harmful practices to involving the population more actively in positive conservation efforts. Speaking at an international conference on trees and forests in Paris in 1986, Sankara emphasized that "our struggle for the trees and the forests is first and foremost a democratic and popular struggle," waged by the people.

Tree-planting initiatives became more pervasive. People were encouraged to plant trees on virtually every family or cultural occasion, from weddings and christenings to the presentation of awards or visits by dignitaries.

Farming families that acquired new tracts of land developed near dams and water reservoirs were each obliged to plant a hundred or more tree seedlings. The traditional village practice of maintaining sacred forests devoted to the ancestors—which fell into disuse with the spread of Christianity and Islam—was partially resurrected under the slogan of "one village, one tree grove." Each community was expected to create a tree nursery to begin reviving protected forest areas in their locale.

State and Market

Reform of the Burkinabè administration was essential not only for enhancing the functioning of the state and its various institutions. Because of the weakness of the country's private sector, the effectiveness of the state was also central for the country's economic development. When Sankara's CNR came to power, it inherited about thirty state-owned enterprises, which included utilities and service agencies as well as firms engaged directly in production, such as gold mining.

These state enterprises, however, were a "poisoned legacy," as the government's *Sidwaya* newspaper put it. They often had very different structures, styles of management, and methods of internal and external control, making it hard for the central authorities to gain a clear picture of their financial position, let alone supervise their functioning. Managers had often given relatives, friends, and political clients jobs in the enterprises, and pilferage and embezzlement became widespread in some of them.

The CNR soon handed over the most grievous cases of outright theft and embezzlement to the People's Revolutionary Tribunals. Many directors and other senior personnel were dismissed for incompetence and negligence, and replaced by others considered more qualified or trustworthy. In 1984 the government decreed a more uniform set of structures, operations, and control mechanisms for all state enterprises. Each was now run on a day-to-day basis by a government-appointed director. Each also had a new administrative council—composed equally of government appointees and representatives of the trade unions and CDRs—that met annually to supervise performance, budgets, investment plans, personnel policies, salary scales, and other matters.

For the first time, the operations of the state enterprises were opened to public scrutiny. In July 1986 and March 1987, public hearings were organized in Ouagadougou's House of the People, at which state enterprise directors, administrative councils, and financial experts had to give an accounting of their performance, financial records, and policies over the previous three years. They did so before large public audiences, as well as some twenty cabinet ministers, sometimes headed by Sankara himself. When state property and interests were at stake, Sankara told the managers, "there can be no sentimentalism." He ordered all directors and senior officers to make full disclosures of their assets. "All personnel must be sensitized to the risks of corruption," he said. "Those who are corrupt and those who corrupt them must be denounced. From now on, failure to expose them will be considered a sign of complicity."

While allowed to operate, private businesses also came under greater scrutiny. They soon found that the era of anything-goes was over. Sankara assured them that they could continue to make money, especially those sectors of "national capital" engaged in direct production. "Private property is a normal thing at this stage of our society. It is normal that it should be protected," he said shortly after taking power. But what could not be accepted, he added, "is private property dishonestly acquired."

Merchants, especially those engaged in hoarding, price-fixing, and various extortionate practices, discovered that the CNR was more energetic than previous regimes in trying to regulate their activities and intervene more directly in market operations. Large businesses had to contend with tax officials demanding that they pay their due share.

However, indigenous producers and entrepreneurs—as against those linked more directly to external capital—gained new opportunities with the CNR's emphasis on building a national economy. Despite the complaints of importers, higher customs duties were imposed to better protect domestic goods from stiff foreign competition.

Under the slogan "Let's produce and consume Burkinabè," the Sankara government also encouraged manufacturers to produce more from local materials and consumers to buy more goods made locally. Bakers were urged to include a small portion of local corn (maize) flour in their bread, rather than just wheat, which was mainly imported. Beverage companies were asked to introduce some sorghum malt in their beer production, and to diversify into bottling mango and other fruit juices. Although modest, such efforts strengthened domestic demand in ways that also gave incentives to farmers to grow more surpluses for commercial sale.

One initiative in particular had multiple economic, social, and political implications—the promotion of dresses, shirts, pants, and other clothing known as Faso dan Fani. In the past, women in traditional villages and in Catholic-run mission stations wove fabrics from local cotton. The practice virtually died out, however, as residents bought more clothes made from imported fabrics and almost all cotton was exported. The CNR acted energetically to revive the manufacture of local clothes. Networks of women weavers were organized in cooperatives to produce Faso dan Fani outfits for both men and women, often in basic blue and white, but also in more elaborate colors and designs. To create a ready market for the clothes, the government obliged all civil servants to wear Faso dan Fani outfits to official ceremonies and events. Some state employees also regularly wore them to work, whether they genuinely liked the outfits or to curry favor with their supervisors, since wearing Faso dan Fani was often portrayed as a patriotic act. Sankara himself frequently wore Faso dan Fani, and he stirred wider interest when he addressed an Organization of African Unity summit in Ethiopia in 1987 in a Faso dan Fani outfit.

For the women who produced the clothes, Faso dan Fani carried more than a political message. It became a major source of revenue, estimated in 1987 at about CFA600 million, or more than US$1 million. That not only gave them additional income but also often enhanced their social status within their families and communities.

7

A Foreign Policy of One's Own

When South African Foreign Minister Pik Botha, one of the most hard-line figures in the apartheid regime, visited Paris in February 1985, Sankara fired off a sharp telegram to his French counterpart. Receiving Botha, he admonished President François Mitterrand, "means strengthening apartheid," adding to the misery of millions of South Africans and delaying the release of Nelson Mandela, the liberation leader imprisoned since 1962. "Receiving Pik Botha is an official way of supporting and legitimizing the most odious crime in the world."

Before the arrival of Sankara's government, such an official protest to the country's former colonial power would have been unthinkable. Upper Volta, like most of France's former colonies in Africa, generally hewed closely to the foreign policy outlook of the authorities in Paris. The French embassy in Ouagadougou was conveniently located right next to the old presidential palace.

Sankara's determination to break from an external policy dictated largely from Paris already had been prefigured in early 1983, during his foreign trips as prime minister in the previous regime, prompting the involvement of French officials in his ouster. After he then became president a few months later, he continued to make bold pronouncements on a wide variety of contentious international topics and more trips to forge new alliances.

True to his frugal ways back home, Sankara ensured that the costs of official travels were kept to a minimum. With no presidential or personal jet at his disposal, he often hitched rides to international meetings with other African heads of state. Now Burkinabè officials traveling abroad were required to fly economy class and stay at the most modest accommodations, including official consular or embassy residences. A staff member of Burkina Faso's UN mission in New York recalled Sankara's 1984 visit there. Mattresses were put on the mission floors for government ministers accompanying him. "There's nothing wrong with that," Sankara told the ministers. "This should bring back to some of you memories from the time you were students." The money saved on hotel bills, he reminded them, would be better used for new wells and schools back home. Such lack of ostentation in Burkinabè officials' travels did not diminish the power of their messages. For some observers, it even enhanced their impact.

From Sankara's numerous declarations on international issues, several themes stand out. First, he sought to establish, in the clearest terms, that Burkina Faso no longer followed direction from Paris—or from

Washington or other Western capitals. Second, as a sovereign nation, Burkina Faso would establish relations with any state it wanted to. Third, in keeping with its revolutionary ideals, the National Council of the Revolution (CNR) would stand in solidarity with oppressed peoples and liberation movements. And finally, it would press for genuine pan-African unity, which Sankara believed could be achieved only through *action* by African governments and peoples, not through an occasional common declaration issued at the close of a summit meeting.

This radically internationalist approach won Burkina Faso new friends in far-flung places and raised its global stature well beyond the country's small size and economic power. It also generated alarm in Western capitals—and among the conservative governments in some of its African neighbors.

Breaking with Tradition

Sankara's face-to-face verbal duel with François Mitterrand in November 1986 (highlighted in chapter 1) was only the most dramatic expression of his government's determination to move away from France's political "sphere of influence." In his October 1984 speech to the United Nations General Assembly, Sankara was implicitly critical of the French military intervention in Chad. He called overtly for the Indian Ocean island of Mayotte, under French control, to be returned to the Comoros, an independent African state. On other occasions, Sankara expressed support for the proindependence Kanak movement that sought an end to French rule over the Pacific territory of New Caledonia.

In November 1984 the Burkinabè minister of trade warned French businesses in the country that the government would no longer maintain "privileged relations" with them, and the finance ministry ordered state banks to briefly suspend financial transfers between those businesses and France. Although Sankara had taken part a year earlier in one of the Franco-African summits that the French government organized periodically with the leaders of its former African colonies, in December 1984 he decided to boycott the next one—and never went to another. A CNR statement explained that the Burkinabè government would participate in international conferences only on the basis of its own economic and political interests. "Our aim is to have the political courage to openly break with an old tradition."

Burkina Faso did attend a February 1986 summit of La Francophonie, a loose cultural grouping of nations that utilize the French language. In a message to the summit read on his behalf by Captain Henri Zongo, Sankara noted that Burkina Faso's use of French was a legacy of its colonial past. Even though only about a tenth of all Burkinabè actually spoke it, the language remained useful for international communication. In his message Sankara observed with some irony that it was through French that he and other Burkinabè revolutionaries learned about the struggle of the Vietnamese people, defended the rights of immigrant workers, read the works of "the great educators of the proletariat," and sung the "Internationale," the song of the world communist movement. If the grouping of Francophone countries was to have any continued relevance, however, it had to acknowledge that there were "two French languages," that spoken within France and "the French language spoken in the five continents." It was a not-so-subtle dig at the efforts of the official Académie Française, supported by the French government, to get French speakers everywhere to conform to the grammar and usage of France itself. Instead, Sankara insisted, the French language—if it was to better serve the democratic ideals of the French revolution of 1789—had to be open to the idioms and concepts of other peoples.

Sankara had traveled to Paris himself a few days before the summit, met François Mitterrand, and signed a series of new cooperation agreements between France and Burkina Faso. On the surface at least, relations between the two countries had eased somewhat, and Sankara's visit to Paris paved the way for Mitterrand to visit Ouagadougou later that year. After Mitterrand's Burkina Faso visit, a journalist asked the French president what new aid France had agreed to provide. He responded, "But President Sankara didn't ask me for anything!"

Earlier, Sankara summarized his government's attitude toward contacts with France: "What is essential is to develop a relationship of equals, mutually beneficial, without paternalism on one side or an inferiority complex on the other."

Sankara's "White House" in Harlem

For the US government, Upper Volta had been a little-known backwater, of no apparent strategic importance to Washington. Although there was a US embassy in Ouagadougou, it mostly oversaw US aid programs and contingents of Peace Corps volunteers. On most political issues, the US authorities seemed content to leave direct involvement to their French counterparts.

According to some accounts, while Sankara was preparing to travel to the United States in 1984 to address the UN General Assembly, the White House asked to see a draft of his planned remarks. The ostensible reason was to consider any possible responses, but it probably was also to determine whether Sankara would be welcome for a White House visit with President Ronald Reagan. Judging the tone of Sankara's draft to be too critical of the major powers, the United States reportedly requested a few alterations. Sankara ignored the request, and no White House invitation was issued. Sankara also was not authorized to stop off in Atlanta, where he had been invited by Mayor Andrew Young, a prominent African American leader.

With his visit limited to New York, Sankara reached out to a different audience. He first spoke publicly before a crowd of more than five hundred African Americans who packed the auditorium of the Harriet Tubman school in Harlem the evening of October 3. It was a relatively short speech that began and ended with a charged litany of call-and-response slogans: "Imperialism," to which the crowd called out, "Down with it!" "Racism," and they shouted, "Down with it!" Sankara's slogan, "Dignity," brought a roar of "To the people!," followed by "Power," and "To the people!" Praising Harlem as a center of Black culture and pride, Sankara asserted that for African revolutionaries, "our White House is in Black Harlem." His words resonated strongly with the audience, especially when he affirmed the connections between the struggles of Africans in Africa and their descendants in the diaspora. Together, he said, they could more strongly fight their common oppressors. When he affirmed that he was "ready for imperialism" and hoisted up his holstered pistol, the audience erupted in laughter and applause. He told them that the next day he would address the United Nations, to speak about injustice, racism, and hypocrisy. "I will tell them that we and you, all of us, are waging our struggles and that they would do well to pay attention."

True to his word, Sankara's speech the following day to the UN General Assembly was hard-hitting and touched on a wide range of global injustices. They spanned the paternalism of Western aid policies and the major powers' armed interventions in poor nations, to the struggle against the apartheid regime in South Africa. Although he was speaking in the United States, he did not mince words when discussing US policies. He said that Burkina Faso stood side by side with the Palestinian struggle "against the armed bands of Israel," a country that for twenty years had defied the international community "with the complicity of its powerful protector, the United States." He condemned the "foreign aggression" against the Caribbean island of Grenada, where the United States had intervened militarily the year before. And he affirmed solidarity with the Sandinista revolutionaries in Nicaragua, "whose harbors are mined, whose villages are bombed," a reference to the "contra" war against Nicaragua supported directly by the Reagan administration.

A Diversity of Relations

As part of its effort to assert greater autonomy from France, Burkina Faso assiduously sought new political, economic, and cultural relations with other countries. Among the traditional donor powers, it signed new aid agreements with the Netherlands, Japan, and Canada. A month after his UN speech, Sankara visited China, which helped build a major sports stadium in Ouagadougou and provided an interest-free loan of $20 million for agricultural development, among other forms of assistance. In 1986 Sankara led a large delegation on a weeklong visit to the Soviet Union, which previously had provided some agricultural equipment, along with other economic assistance. Such Soviet aid did not keep Sankara from publicly criticizing the Soviet military intervention in

Afghanistan, which he did in his UN speech and on other occasions. Nor did Sankara's earlier relations with Libya prevent the Burkinabè government from publicly criticizing the mediocre quality of Libyan assistance.

Sankara exhibited a strong personal affinity for Cuba. After his speech as prime minister at the Non-Aligned summit in New Delhi in March 1983, Cuban president Fidel Castro invited him to his suite one evening to get to know him better, and the two became friendly. Just a few months after the CNR was established, in December 1983, Burkina Faso signed a scientific, economic, and technical cooperation agreement with Cuba. Under it, Cuba sent some two dozen medical personnel to Burkina Faso and provided aid in agriculture, economic planning, stockbreeding, transportation, education, and dam construction. On his way to New York for the UN General Assembly, Sankara first stopped off in Cuba, where he was awarded the Order of José Martí, Cuba's highest honor. In accepting it, Sankara remarked, "Cuba and Burkina Faso are so far and yet so near, so different and yet so similar, that only revolutionaries can understand the sincere love that pushes us irresistibly toward one another." In November 1986 Sankara traveled once again to Cuba, where he met with Castro twice.

From Cuba, Sankara made a short side trip to Nicaragua, returning a visit that Nicaraguan president Daniel Ortega had made to Burkina Faso three months earlier. In Nicaragua, Sankara spoke to a crowd of two hundred thousand on behalf of all foreign delegations attending a celebration of the twenty-fifth anniversary of the ruling Sandinista National Liberation Front, which had overthrown a US-backed dictatorship seven years earlier. As he did in his UN speech, Sankara expressed solidarity with Nicaragua in face of the US-supported "contra" war.

The CNR's decision to establish new ties with a range of governments that were generally at odds with Paris and Washington stirred some critical reactions from those powers. "People accuse us of being the pawn of Libya, Cuba, the USSR, and Algeria," Sankara noted. He denied that accusation, and dismissed the notion that the CNR was copying those political models. "The Burkinabè revolution is not an imported revolution."

Challenging African Leaders

Sankara was a strong champion of pan-African unity and the principles of the then Organization of African Unity (OAU, now the African Union). Yet he held no illusions about the willingness or ability of most African leaders to take concerted action in defense of the continent's common interests. At annual summit meetings of the OAU and in his frequent trips in Africa, he often prodded and cajoled his peers to match their conference speeches with concrete deeds.

The struggle for freedom in South Africa and Namibia was the issue on which he was most persistent. The seeming intractability of the apartheid regime—despite international sanctions and near-universal condemnation within Africa—was an affront to all Africans, Sankara believed. As long as the basic rights of the majority of South Africans and Namibians were denied, Africa as a whole could not achieve true unity or advance economically and politically.

One of the earliest acts of Sankara's CNR was to rename a central thoroughfare in the capital Nelson Mandela Avenue. The government symbolically issued Mandela a Burkinabè passport, in effect claiming him as a citizen. Of more practical effect, South African goods were barred from sale in Burkina Faso. Local activists mounted a campaign against Shell Oil, one of the country's main oil suppliers, as part of an international boycott of the company for its dealings in South Africa, and the Sankara government responded by exploring arrangements with alternative suppliers. Encouraged by frequent Burkinabè media accounts of the horrors of apartheid and the struggles of the African National Congress (ANC) in South Africa and the South West Africa People's Organization (SWAPO) in Namibia, a number of local antiapartheid committees emerged, based largely at the university and secondary schools.

In many of his speeches on international issues, Sankara cited the importance of the Southern African freedom struggles and the need to make sanctions against the apartheid regime more effective. At an OAU summit in 1986 he publicly offered ten rifles to ANC and SWAPO fighters. As some African leaders started to chuckle, Sankara continued, "Ten rifles represent something really big to a poor country like Burkina Faso." He then challenged the other OAU leaders: "If every one of the fifty OAU states did the same, it would mean that 500 African National Congress or South West Africa People's Organization soldiers would be armed."

Though couched in military terms, Sankara's real point was political. If African countries actually took some action—rather than limit themselves to flowery speeches and impassioned denunciations—then the movement in solidarity with the Southern African freedom struggles might make more headway. That was the main theme of a pan-African antiapartheid conference held in Ouagadougou October 8–11, 1987 (just a few days before the coup). The Bambata Forum—named after an early South African rebel—had the government's blessing, but was mainly organized and financed by local activist groups. Most of the deliberations focused on how people in various African countries could mobilize support for the ANC and SWAPO without necessarily relying on their governments to take action.

Another struggle within Africa that Sankara championed was that of the independence movement in Western Sahara. It was originally a colony of Spain, which relinquished control in 1975 to Morocco and Mauritania; a few years later Mauritania withdrew, and Morocco occupied the remaining territory as well. That occupation, however,

Sankara at a pan-African antiapartheid conference in Ouagadougou just a few days before his death. Supporting the liberation movements in Southern Africa was a keystone of his foreign policy. *Credit: Ernest Harsch*

encountered the resistance of a movement known as the Polisario Front, which proclaimed its own state, the Sahrawi Arab Democratic Republic (SADR). The Burkinabè government officially recognized the SADR, and at the end of March 1984 Sankara became the first head of state to visit areas of Western Sahara under the control of the Polisario Front. He then pushed strongly within the OAU for wider recognition of the SADR. Before the year was out, the OAU did officially admit the Sahrawi republic, prompting Morocco's withdrawal from the organization and irritating France, which generally supported Morocco's claim to the territory.

At the time, one of the most burning economic issues confronting Africa was the continent's enormous foreign debt, some $200 billion in 1986. The annual payments on those debts, generally owed to Western donor agencies, banks, and financial institutions, consumed about 40 percent of African countries' export earnings, on average. That left little for essential imports and basic services, let alone development. Individual African countries, and since 1984 the OAU itself, pleaded with creditors for some relief. But only small portions of Africa's debts were forgiven, with creditors usually agreeing only to postpone payments somewhat. In exchange for even that, they insisted on strict domestic austerity measures, which in some countries led to serious rioting and political instability.

Believing that African leaders' entreaties to Western creditors were too timid, Sankara made a bold proposal at a July 1987 summit of the OAU: that Africa, collectively, simply refuse to pay. He cited two arguments. First, African countries just did not have the money to keep up repayments without plunging their economies and peoples into even deeper crises. "We cannot repay the debt because we have nothing to pay it with." Second, many African countries originally took the loans, at steep interest rates, on the advice of Western financial experts, who ultimately bore responsibility for the mushrooming of the debt. "Those who led us into debt were gambling, as if they were in a casino. As long as they were winning, there was no problem. Now that they're losing their bets, they demand repayment." Individually, African countries would be too weak to refuse to pay, Sankara pointed out. So he proposed that African leaders stand together and create a "united front" against the debt. The OAU never followed Sankara's advice, although at the end of that year it did adopt a common position on the debt proposing a "constructive dialogue" to reduce Africa's debt payments to "reasonable and bearable" levels.

Ripples in the Neighborhood

Of all countries in its immediate region, the Sankara government enjoyed the closest relations with Ghana. Those dated back to when Sankara was prime minister in early 1983. The year before, radical junior military officers, led by Flight Lieutenant Jerry John Rawlings, allied with civilian leftist groups and seized power in Ghana, proclaiming

Sankara with President Jerry Rawlings of Ghana. Among West African leaders, the two were especially close political allies. *Credit: Service de la presse présidentielle/Bara*

their own revolutionary and anti-imperialist intentions. Prime Minister Sankara commented at a mass rally in Ouagadougou in March 1983: "When Rawlings says, 'No way for kalabule!'—that is, stop the corruption—he says this in the interests of the Ghanaian people. But in fact it is in the interests of all peoples, because the Voltaic people too are against corruption." After Sankara was ousted as prime minister and his supporters established a base of resistance in Pô, they made clandestine contacts with the Rawlings government in Ghana, whose border was only 20 kilometers south of Pô.

Just a little more than a month after the radicals took power in Ouagadougou, Rawlings himself traveled to Pô to meet with Sankara. In February 1984 he returned for a large welcoming rally in Ouagadougou. On that occasion, Sankara publicly revealed that Rawlings had "dared to support us with all his military, political, and diplomatic strength" during the period leading up to the CNR's triumph. By that point, Burkinabè and Ghanaian military forces had already organized a series of joint military maneuvers, codenamed Bold Union, to dramatically signal their mutual solidarity. They organized a second, longer set of joint maneuvers in 1985. According to Sankara, the affinity was based on a common "spirit of liberty and dignity, of counting on one's own resources, of independence, and of consistent anti-imperialist struggle."

Of Burkina Faso's other immediate neighbors, relations with Benin, which was headed by a left-leaning government that had its own conflicts with France, were moderately warm, while those with Niger were usually relatively cordial. However, political contacts with the three other countries with which Burkina Faso shared a common border—Togo, Mali, and Côte d'Ivoire— were generally tense. All were politically close to France, gave sanctuary to Burkinabè opponents of the Sankara government, and were worried about the potential for revolutionary contagion. When they experienced domestic opposition, they often pointed a finger of blame at Ouagadougou, as the Togolese government did after a failed coup attempt in 1986.

Some analysts saw the Malian government's decision to provoke the brief December 1985 border war with

Burkina Faso as motivated, at least in part, by a fear that Sankara's popularity among some sectors within Mali could lead to overt challenges. Sankara may have stoked that concern to some extent. In a September 1985 speech to a mass rally in Ouagadougou in which he took up various threats against the CNR from the region's more conservative governments, Sankara pointedly stated, "The revolution of the Burkinabè people is at the disposal of the people of Mali, who need it. . . . Only revolution will allow them to free themselves."

The government of neighboring Côte d'Ivoire was similarly nervous about developments next door—an anxiety heightened by the fact that up to 2 million Burkinabè lived and worked there. President Félix Houphouët-Boigny, who had governed that country since independence in 1960, was one of France's closet allies in Africa. In November 1984 Côte d'Ivoire hosted its largest-ever joint military exercises with France, involving two thousand French and three thousand Ivorian troops and assorted jet fighters and helicopter gun ships. It was not necessary to make any overt threats against the CNR. The message of the exercises was clear: they were held by the Comoé River, along the border between Côte d'Ivoire and Burkina Faso.

Given Côte d'Ivoire's economic and political weight in the region and the presence of large numbers of Burkinabè citizens in that country, the Sankara government was careful in its dealings with President Houphouët-Boigny. It was not easy. A first planned visit by Sankara to Côte d'Ivoire in May 1984 was cancelled when the Ivorian government refused to let Sankara visit Abidjan, the largest city, apparently out of concern over the welcome he might receive from its inhabitants. A visit was finally organized the following February, not in Abidjan, but in the political capital, Yamoussoukro, a much smaller town. Some eighteen hours before Sankara's arrival, a bomb exploded in the hotel suite where he was supposed to stay. But the visit went ahead anyway, and Sankara met with Houphouët-Boigny. Though it was not Abidjan, thousands of Ivorians and Burkinabè nevertheless turned out to greet Sankara.

On the surface at least, relations between the two governments remained proper. In 1986, Houphouët-Boigny visited Ouagadougou and was given a cordial welcome. As he had done in several other countries in West Africa, the Ivorian president also put out feelers to potential political allies within Burkina Faso. He scored a notable advance in this when in June 1985 Chantal Terrasson de Fougères, who was raised in Houphouët-Boigny's household as an adopted daughter, married the Burkinabè minister of defense—Captain Blaise Compaoré.

8

The Last Battles

The day of the coup that ended Sankara's life, October 15, 1987, I was in the small village of Pibaoré, a hundred or so kilometers northeast of Ouagadougou. Like others in rural Burkina Faso, the residents of Pibaoré could point to tangible changes: a recently formed peasants' union, a brick schoolhouse, a cereal bank for surplus grain, literacy classes, several thousand newly planted trees, a water reservoir, and improved harvests of millet and sorghum. They had rallied in Pibaoré's central square to celebrate those achievements. A few younger participants wore T-shirts bearing Sankara's image. As elsewhere, the inhabitants of Pibaoré identified the revolution with their president. "He doesn't just make promises, like the old politicians," one commented. "He gets things done." A moment's thought, and then he added, "He's shown us that we can get things done."

After the rally ended, some youths listening to Radio Ouagadougou started to hear military music rather than the normal programming. They were puzzled. Then sometime between 5 and 6 p.m. came a stunning announcement: "patriotic forces" in Ouagadougou had brought an end to "the autocratic power of Thomas Sankara." The day's celebratory mood first turned to disbelief, then to grief and sadness.

The next morning, back in Ouagadougou, I learned what everyone there already knew: Sankara had been not only overthrown, but also killed. The radio broadcast very little hard information—not even an official announcement of Sankara's death. It reported only that the National Council of the Revolution (CNR), government, and a few other institutions had been dissolved and replaced by a mysterious "Popular Front," headed by a new president, Captain Blaise Compaoré. The airwaves were also filled with invective. Sankara was vilified as a "traitor" to the revolution, a "petty-bourgeois" who "consorted with bourgeois potentates" and was guided by "mystic forces," a "messianic" who ran a "one-man show," a "fascist," even a "paranoiac misogynist."

Few people I spoke with in Ouagadougou believed the accusations. Many found them quite distasteful. They were also disgusted when they learned that Sankara and twelve comrades slain with him had been buried unceremoniously, with no grave markers, in Dagnoën cemetery, on the edge of one of the capital's poorer neighborhoods. As news of the location spread by word of mouth, first small groups and then hundreds trekked by foot to the cemetery to lay flowers on the grave mounds and to weep.

Captain Blaise Compaoré (*left*), who seized the presidency after Sankara's assassination, with Commander Jean-Baptiste Lingani and Captain Henri Zongo a year after the coup. Lingani and Zongo were summarily executed in 1989. *Credit: Ernest Harsch*

How did this stunning turn of events happen? How could one of Sankara's closest comrades—and personal friends—carry out such a bloody coup? For some months, there had been rumors of divergences within the revolutionary leadership but few clear explanations of what the differences entailed. I last spoke with Sankara four days before his death, and he gave no hint of serious problems. One of his aides—Frédéric Kiemdé, who was to die in the same fusillade—did confide that there were disagreements over issues of political organization and the use of repression against government critics. Yet no one seemed to expect such a dramatic outcome. Only in retrospect was it possible to piece together a plausible explanation of some of the factors that contributed to the assassination and coup.

From Outside and Within

Sankara's revolutionary project obviously had external enemies, and a number of analysts pointed to the likelihood of foreign involvement in the 1987 coup. France stood at the top of the list of suspects, a natural assumption given its previous part in the ouster of Sankara as prime minister in early 1983. So far, no solid evidence has emerged indicating a direct French role in the 1987 coup, although Jacques Foccart, a key French intelligence figure with extensive networks of influence throughout Africa, was known to be hostile to Sankara and may well have encouraged regional allies to make a move. The governments of Togo and Mali were closely allied with France and openly supported Burkinabè opponents of Sankara's CNR. But it was the regime in Côte d'Ivoire that was best positioned to foment a coup from within, especially with President Houphouët-Boigny's growing ties with Compaoré. Some also suspected that Libya's Qaddafi may have been implicated, since his relations with Sankara had become somewhat strained and his post-coup ties with Compaoré were markedly warm. Two Liberian warlords (Prince Johnson and John Tarnue) later stated publicly that they had been asked to help Compaoré oust Sankara, although details of their accounts were contradictory.

Whatever the nature or extent of foreign involvement in the coup, the most compelling—and troubling—evidence pointed to domestic forces. Not only were the immediate perpetrators Burkinabè, but they came from among Sankara's collaborators in the CNR, government, and military command.

Historically, revolutions and revolutionary efforts worldwide have often been beset by internal differences and conflicts. Frequently even minor divergences have widened under the pressures of domestic opposition and a hostile external environment. As an avid student of revolutions, Sankara was quite conscious of such dangers. He was also well aware that over time revolutionary leaderships may abandon their original ideals; lose touch with their people; become more hardened, inward-looking, and repressive; and succumb to corruption and self-interest. In a number of public statements, especially during the last two years of his life, Sankara seemed particularly concerned that such a fate could be in store for Burkina Faso. He urged diligence and corrective measures "to prevent the revolution from turning in on itself, to prevent the revolution from ossifying, to prevent the revolution from shriveling up like a dried fig."

Between Coercion and Persuasion

In trying to advance the revolutionary process, Sankara had not hesitated to use repressive means when that seemed necessary. He favored firm action against those who directly opposed the government or who engaged in activities considered threatening to political stability. The dangers were not imagined. In 1984 Colonel Didier Tiendrébéogo, several other officers, and some civilian collaborators were caught plotting a coup; a military court acquitted more than a dozen, but ordered the execution of the leaders. In 1985 saboteurs blew up army ammunition depots in Ouagadougou and Bobo-Dioulasso, taking several lives. An army captain suspected of those attacks fled the country and was later detected by Burkinabè intelligence among the Malian forces that attacked Burkina Faso that December.

As the CNR gradually consolidated its position and overt security challenges were contained, Sankara shifted focus. He increasingly found himself trying to discipline those within the military, police, state bureaucracy, and Committees for the Defense of the Revolution (CDRs) who used their repressive powers arbitrarily, against potential allies or even ordinary citizens. Sankara drew a distinction: "While the revolution means repression of the exploiters, of our enemies, it must mean only persuasion for the masses—persuasion to take on a conscious and determined commitment."

Initially, some of the greatest problems came from a layer of activists in the CDRs. Some went to extremes against perceived enemies, ordering beatings and arbitrary arrests. In 1984 the offices of the only private newspaper, *L'Observateur,* were burned down, many suspected by zealous militants. Abusing their positions as representatives of the CNR, some CDR members wielded authority not in defense of the revolution but to lord it over others, get back at personal enemies, and engage in extortion. Some embezzled funds or broke into people's homes. Among the armed members of the CDRs' vigilance brigades, a few used their weapons for shakedowns and armed robberies. Such activities alienated people from the CDRs and stained the image of the government and CNR. Years later, many Burkinabè remembered the misdeeds of the CDRs even more than the successes of their popular mobilizations.

As early as a month after coming to power, Sankara recognized the potential danger of the CDRs' repressive powers, acknowledging "a risk of seeing them degenerate." By late 1985, a few of the most extreme cases of "gangster CDRs" were brought to trial before the People's Revolutionary Tribunals. Then early the next year many frank self-criticisms were aired at the first national conference of CDRs. Sankara, in the closing address, was especially scathing. Some CDR leaders, he said, had "set themselves up as veritable despots in the local districts, in the villages, and in the provinces. . . . [r]eigning and holding sway like warlords." Sankara admonished them: "The CDR office must not be a locale of torturers but the complete opposite: an office where you find people who lead, who organize, who mobilize, who educate, and who struggle as revolutionaries."

Subsequently, many CDRs were reorganized and un-disciplined leaders purged. The security functions of the CDRs were downgraded, with fewer armed patrols and other operations by their vigilance brigades. However, the absence of alternative mechanisms of expression outside the CDRs made it hard to keep them in check.

The CDRs were not the only institutions that leaned toward coercion when faced with dissidence. The government and CNR also reacted with a heavy hand, at least initially with Sankara's apparent approval. The repression started with the detention of leaders of the old elite political parties but eventually extended to some of those originally seen as revolutionary allies.

Relations with the trade unions, especially those in the public sector, soured over the dismissal of state employees. Some were let go because of incompetence but others because they were suspected of political disloyalty, sometimes for little more than past party affiliations. Most dramatically, a serious conflict developed between the CNR and the main primary school teachers union, led by supporters of Joseph Ki-Zerbo, an internationally known historian, then living in exile in Senegal, who had been close to the previous military regime of Colonel Saye Zerbo. In March 1984 the authorities ordered the arrest of several of the teachers' leaders. That prompted a three-day protest strike, to which the Ministry of Education responded by dismissing some 1,300 teachers. Many Burkinabè were shocked by the severity of the reaction.

That same year, political differences within the CNR and government led to the ejection of supporters of the African Independence Party (PAI). One of the group's best-known leaders, Soumane Touré, also led a major labor federation, so the rift further strained relations with the unions. Over the next three years, Touré and other unionists were repeatedly detained. Matters came to a head in May 1987 when members of a CDR in Ouagadougou again arrested Touré, along with several others. Accusing them of planning antigovernment protests, the CDR publicly called for their execution, an especially provocative act since Sankara and Touré were known to be personal friends. Kiemdé, Sankara's aide, told me that Sankara opposed the detentions as damaging to the revolution. He quietly pressed for their release, and several of the lesser-known detainees were freed. Within the CNR Sankara also fought to block the executions—which were favored by all but one of the political groups in the council. The loudest calls for execution came from the Union of Burkinabè Communists, which was close to Blaise Compaoré. According to Valère Somé, who sided with the president, Sankara's intervention in the CNR "was decisive in saving Soumane Touré's life." Sankara later told a group of journalists that because of his stance, "There's now a campaign against me. I'm accused of being a sentimentalist."

Sankara's position on Touré's case was motivated not just by friendship. It reflected a broader shift during 1986 and 1987 to try to ease up on coercion and reduce social tensions. A number of the imprisoned officials of previous governments were let go, and several hundred of the dismissed teachers were rehired. Two months before the coup, Sankara urged the reintegration of more teachers and instructed all cabinet ministers to find ways to reinstate civil servants who had been fired for political reasons. Sankara also announced a "pause" in efforts to carry out various projects, an apparent acknowledgment of the signs of fatigue exhibited by sectors of the population over the frenetic pace of the CNR's social mobilizations.

Repeatedly, Sankara tried to persuade his comrades that the revolution could advance only if people were won over to its goals, of their own free will, not through compulsion. The revolution, he said, "needs a convinced people, not a conquered people—a convinced people, not a submissive people passively enduring their fate." The aim should be to win over everyone. "We are eight million Burkinabè; our goal is to create eight million revolutionaries." Failing to rely on persuasion, he said just before the coup, would inevitably lead to yet more repression: "A conquered people means an endless series of prisons. . . . For revolutionaries, victory lies in the disappearance of prisons. For reactionaries, victory lies in the construction of a maximum number of prisons. That's the difference between them and us."

"Rich with a Thousand Nuances"

Sankara's views on coercion related closely to his thinking on the kind of political organization that could best move the revolutionary process forward. Many of his colleagues focused on how to best unify the disparate leftist groups that supported the CNR—and usually maneuvered to try to position their own organization in the lead. Sankara, however, regarded the existing groups as too narrow and self-absorbed. He repeatedly emphasized opening up to broader sectors of the population, starting with the many activists not affiliated with the established political groups.

When the CNR came to power in August 1983, there were two civilian organizations allied with Sankara's radical military current: the PAI, which operated publicly as the League for Patriotic Development (Lipad); and the Union of Communist Struggle-Reconstructed (ULCR), led by Valère Somé. The ULCR's support did not extend much beyond students, professors, and other professionals. The PAI/Lipad had a notable base in the unions. Sankara and most of the other officers in the CNR constituted themselves as the Revolutionary Military Organization (OMR). Following the expulsion of the PAI/Lipad from the CNR and government in 1984, three other groups emerged and joined the CNR: the Union of Communist Struggle (ULC), the Burkinabè Communist Group (GCB), and the Union of Burkinabè Communist (UCB). All were very small, with roots mainly in the student movement and among academics and media personnel. The UCB also had support from sectors of the officer corps, leading some of its rivals to label it "militarist." Most of these groups' leaders were ideological disciples of Stalin,

Mao, or Enver Hoxha (of Albania), reflecting their dogmatic, intolerant views.

In 1986, all the political formations in the CNR signed an agreement to dissolve themselves as separate groups and merge into a united political party. But the negotiations were bogged down by ideological differences, personal rivalries, sectarianism, and divisive factional maneuvers, including by Compaoré and other officers. Sankara was in favor of exploring renewed ties with the PAI/Lipad, but any overtures were cut short by the May 1987 arrest of Soumane Touré, seemingly at the UCB's instigation. The ULCR, which often sided with Sankara, also found itself under attack by the UCB and the other groups, with some of its activists at the University of Ouagadougou even detained by soldiers.

Sankara tried to mediate among the factions, largely in vain. He also tried to get them to look beyond their own organizational identities, to keep in mind the real issue that concerned most Burkinabè: bettering their daily lives. He made it clear that he favored unification of the various revolutionary currents, but not through a narrow, mechanical merger of the established groups. "Our democratic and popular revolution sets itself aside from all sects and sectarian groupings," he said. To think that "only a certain nucleus, only a certain group, is worth anything" would end up isolating the leadership. Sankara warned that creating a political vanguard through a simple amalgamation of existing organizations could lead to a "nomenklatura of untouchable dignitaries," using the Russian word for a Soviet-style list of state positions reserved solely for party appointees.

Above all, Sankara insisted, a revolutionary organization should be open to many viewpoints. It was necessary to "guard against making unity into a dry, paralyzing, sterilizing, monochromatic thing. On the contrary, we would rather see a manifold, varied, and enriching expression of many different ideas and diverse activities, ideas and activities that are rich with a thousand nuances."

Fighting the "Gangrene of Corruption"

Besides pressing on issues of coercion and organization, Sankara also sought to reinvigorate the battle against corruption. In his government's early years that struggle concentrated mainly on politicians and functionaries from the previous administrations, through the trials before the People's Revolutionary Tribunals (TPRs). Now the emphasis was to be on *current* officeholders. Sankara was concerned about corruption not just among ordinary civil servants or CDR activists, but most especially among members of his own leadership team. Just a few days before the coup, Sankara told a group of journalists that "today there are people in power who live better lives than the population, who engage in small-scale trade with Syrian-Lebanese merchants, who find positions for their families, their younger cousins, all the while speaking in very revolutionary language."

According to Fidèle Toé, who was minister of labor at the time, one of Sankara's last acts was to propose a "revolutionary code of conduct." He first introduced the idea at a council of ministers meeting chaired by Compaoré on October 7, 1987, and then led a discussion of the topic at an October 14 council meeting (chaired by Sankara and in Compaoré's absence). The broad outlines of such a code, Toé later recounted, were to ensure that all leadership cadres had the endurance and intellectual capacity to fulfill their responsibilities and conducted themselves with honesty, integrity, and "revolutionary morality."

The most important measure to try to ensure such morality had come earlier that year. In February Sankara established the People's Commission for the Prevention of Corruption (CPPC). Its main purpose was to collect and investigate information on the incomes and assets of all high officials to see whether they were living beyond their means. Any anomalies were to be passed on to the police for further investigation, and if there was evidence of a possible crime, the perpetrator would be charged before a TPR. The CPPC's function, said a CNR declaration, was to help "preserve our society and our revolution from the gangrene of corruption, a weapon used by imperialism and the bourgeoisie to lead astray revolutions from within."

Sankara was the first to appear before the CPPC. According to his declaration of assets, he owned one house, on which he was still paying a mortgage, two undeveloped plots of land, an automobile, several bicycles, a refrigerator, kitchen appliances, and several guitars. His monthly salary was CFA136,736 (equivalent to US$462 at the time), while his wife's was CFA192,690. Their combined bank accounts totaled just CFA532,127. He also reported that foreign leaders had given him gifts while traveling abroad, including four cars and more than CFA850 million in cash, all of which as a matter of policy he had handed over to the state treasury.

After his declaration, Sankara noted in an interview with a Burkinabè newspaper that while the earlier efforts to punish corruption through the TPRs were extremely important, those accomplishments remained "very fragile." He continued: "Every day we are tempted by corruption. People come and offer us opportunities. They often come in the guise of caring. They promise you this or that. They even try to convince you that it's in the interests of the country that they come to praise you and offer you a gift. We are tempted to take it." He hoped that mechanisms such as the CPPC would help his comrades avoid being corrupted, knowing that some day they might have to give an accounting.

Publicly, Sankara denied that he had any specific comrades in mind. But some of his colleagues later recalled that he sometimes expressed concern about the influence of Chantal Terrasson de Fougères, Compaoré's wife, who made little secret of her taste for luxuries. Compaoré himself was "not very enthusiastic about the struggle against corruption," Ernest Nongma Ouédraogo, who was then interior minister, later explained to me. After declaring his own assets, according to Ouédraogo, Compaoré was subsequently "reproached for having hidden certain properties of his wife, such as a massive gold clock given to her by President Houphouët-Boigny" of Côte d'Ivoire.

It would be unfair to pin too much blame on Compaoré's wife. He was known to be politically ambitious. As early as August 1983, just before the advent of the CNR, Compaoré reportedly told one of Sankara's security aides that he, Compaoré, would be president and Sankara prime minister. Once Sankara and the other leaders learned of that position, they collectively "clarified" who among them would be the best face of the new government. Frustrated at the outset, Compaoré may have viewed his marriage to someone from Houphouët-Boigny's family as a step toward a beneficial future alliance.

Revenge of the Elites

Whatever the weight of individual ambition or corruption in the developments that led to Sankara's death, it is likely that the coup plotters also counted on support (tacit or otherwise) from wider segments of disgruntled social layers. All those who lost some of their powers and privileges as a result of Sankara's revolutionary venture—the social elites, land speculators, big merchants, traditional chiefs—had good reason to see him go. In the months leading to the coup, anonymous leaflets circulated in Ouagadougou and other cities calling on Mossi to unite against the government of the "stranger," an implicit rallying cry in favor of Compaoré, a Mossi, and against a non-Mossi president who had sought to curtail the authority of the predominantly Mossi traditional chiefs.

Within the state bureaucracy itself, there were many senior civil servants, public functionaries, and military officers who did not see why they should have to make sacrifices to free up funds for rural development. They resented the trimming of their bonuses and resisted efforts to reassign them to provincial towns, far from the capital's relative comforts. The CNR's stern anticorruption measures stymied their aspirations for self-enrichment.

Sankara recognized the risks of challenging this layer. In a 1985 interview, he told me: "The revolution in Africa faces a big danger, since it is initiated every time by the petty bourgeoisie. The petty bourgeoisie is generally made up of intellectuals. At the beginning of the revolution the big bourgeoisie is attacked. That's easy. . . . But after one, two, or three years, it's necessary to take on the petty bourgeoisie. And when we take on the petty bourgeoisie, we take on the very leadership of the revolution. . . . To take on the petty bourgeoisie means keeping the revolution radical, and there you will face many difficulties. Or you can go easy on the petty bourgeoisie. You won't have any difficulties. But then it won't be a revolution either—it will be a pseudorevolution."

"It's Me They Want"

On the morning of Thursday, October 15, 1987, Sankara met for several hours with Valère Somé at the presidential residence to discuss various matters. The most pressing among them, according to Somé, concerned the ongoing strains between Sankara and Compaoré and among the various political currents within the leadership. Also that morning, Sankara drafted a speech to a meeting of the Revolutionary Military Organization to be held that evening. In it he proposed a "purification" of the CNR and implementation of the code of conduct, among other measures, so as to dispel the "distrust and suspicion" that were infecting the revolution's supporters and lessen the "factionalism" among its leaders. But it was a speech he would never get to deliver.

That afternoon, Sankara had a scheduled meeting with his small team of advisers. They gathered about 4:15 p.m. at the old Conseil de l'Entente headquarters, which for some time had served as an office of the CNR. The meeting was under way for only a brief time when shooting erupted in the small courtyard outside, around 4:30 p.m. or shortly after. Sankara's driver and two of his bodyguards were the first to be killed. Upon hearing the gunfire, everyone in the meeting room quickly took cover. Sankara then got up and told his aides to stay inside for their own safety. "It's me they want." He left the room, hands raised, to face the assailants. He was shot several times, and died without saying anything more. If his exit from the room was intended to save his comrades inside, it failed. The gunmen, all in military uniform, entered the meeting room and sprayed it with automatic weapons fire. Everyone inside was killed, except for Alouna Traoré,

Villagers rallying in Pibaoré in support of the Sankara government, shortly before Sankara's assassination later that day. *Credit: Ernest Harsch*

who survived his wounds and later gave the only eyewitness account of the attack.

Compaoré denied that he had issued orders for Sankara's assassination, and claimed to have been at home in bed ill at the time of the killing. Many found it hard to believe that his men would have acted on their own. And they *were* Compaoré's men. The killers included Sergeant Hyacinthe Kafando, Compaoré's aide de camp. He and the other known assailants all served directly under Captain Gilbert Diendéré, then the commander of the Pô commando base and soon to become head of Compaoré's military security force.

Because of their actions, Compaoré was no longer just the number two. By that evening, he was the new president.

9

"Is It Possible to Forget You?"

Some months before the October 1987 coup, a colleague of mine presented to Sankara my proposal for a book of speeches, interviews, and other documents from the revolutionary process in Burkina Faso. Sankara liked the overall idea. But he objected that the proposal focused too much on him. "The story of our revolution needs to be told, so that the world can know what we are trying to achieve," he told my colleague. "But I am not this revolution, and cannot be the only one to carry this revolution. If this is the case, then we don't have a revolution."

Reflecting on those comments in the aftermath of Sankara's death—and the evident collapse of much of the popular initiative that had given momentum to the changes he tried to carry out—it seemed that Sankara had been too optimistic. He was correct in one sense: it was not just about him. Many tens of thousands of Burkinabè found inspiration in the revolutionary venture, and gained some confidence that the leadership was serious about bringing fundamental improvements. Yet ultimately, that leadership proved to be quite thin.

Among the top leaders, few other than Sankara demonstrated a clear ability to inspire popular support. Only Valère Somé and several others belonging to the ULCR and OMR openly stood with him in the contentious debates that divided the CNR. If the issues in dispute had been pursued solely through political discussion—and taken before the public—it is possible Sankara might yet have prevailed. But his most determined opponents worked in the shadows, through conspiratorial means, not in the arena of contending political ideas. Within the military itself, the plotters managed to take those officers and men who were loyal to Sankara off guard, and arrested many. A garrison in Koudougou led by Captain Boukary Kaboré refused to recognize Compaoré's new Popular Front government, but its defiance was suppressed by force, with the loss of many lives and Kaboré's flight to neighboring Ghana.

This is not the book to recount what happened in the wake of the coup or to analyze the nature of the new regime and its policies. It is enough to note that Compaoré's initial claim that he was trying to "rectify" the revolution and set it back on track soon proved hollow. From the outset the new authorities enjoyed very little popular support. Beyond the tiny political groups that participated in the coup, they relied mainly on backing from the social elites, bureaucrats, merchants, traditional chiefs, and leaders of the old parties of the 1960s and 1970s. Within a few years, even the paper-thin veneer of revolutionary rhetoric was peeled away. Politics increasingly revolved around material favors, corruption, and outright repression. Various human rights groups catalogued the detention or killing of scores of political dissidents, student activists, journalists, and ordinary citizens over the years. Norbert Zongo, the country's leading investigative journalist, was assassinated with three colleagues in 1998, apparently by members of the elite presidential guard. The majority of Burkinabè remained mired in poverty. In 2012, according to the United Nations, the level of "human development" in Burkina Faso was the fifth lowest in the world.

Meanwhile, in the wake of the coup, relations with Burkina Faso's more conservative neighbors, especially the governments of Côte d'Ivoire and Togo, grew close. Ties with France improved markedly. The French authorities not only regularly welcomed Compaoré to Paris but even awarded their National Order of the Legion of Honor to Colonel (later General) Gilbert Diendéré, the officer who commanded Sankara's executioners.

So what was left of Sankara's revolution? The most obvious answer is: the memory of the man, and the ideas he so passionately defended.

Thousands of Burkinabè expressed their deep emotional attachment to Sankara in the days immediately after his death. They walked to the Dagnoën cemetery to pay their respects at his graveside. Some laid flowers and wept. Others left handwritten messages: "Long live the president of the poor." "The jealous, power-hungry, and traitors murdered you." "Mama Sankara, your son will be avenged. We are all Sankara." "Is it possible to forget you?" "A hero never dies."

In the first few years after the coup, it was very risky for any Burkinabè to publicly proclaim their admiration for the late president. Many who had worked closely with Sankara or refused to support the new regime were detained, beaten, or driven into exile. Commander Jean-Baptiste Lingani and Captain Henri Zongo, the two other surviving "historic" military leaders of the CNR's seizure of power, were summarily executed in 1989. Although they had not backed Sankara two years earlier, neither were they active in Compaoré's coup; they thus were suspect.

By the start of the 1990s, domestic opposition built up and spilled into the streets with calls for greater freedom. That opposition, combined with pressure from donors, obliged the government to grudgingly allow multiparty elections. Compaoré's party—with direct access to state resources, financing from business, and some fraud— easily dominated the elections. But the slightly greater openness of the political system also made it possible for new parties to arise. A dozen or more groups identifying themselves as "Sankarist" eventually organized and won legal recognition. Some fielded candidates in elections, often citing Sankara's example and his ideas to attract votes. The various Sankarist parties consistently won a notable minority of the electorate, rising from more than

100,000 votes in 2002 to nearly twice that in 2012. Despite their disunity, these Sankarists managed to elect a handful of deputies to parliament and to stand out as a distinct voice among a plethora of opposition forces.

Attitudes in favor of Sankara extended far beyond the electoral arena—kept alive by widespread dissatisfaction with political and social conditions in the country. Young people, artists, musicians, and activists often recalled his ideas, and during times of crisis in particular protesters often held up his portrait or shouted slogans from Sankara's revolutionary era.

As early as 1991, the strength of this pro-Sankara sentiment obliged the government to officially acknowledge him as a "national hero." Yet it continued to refuse calls for a judicial inquiry into his death. Then in the wake of a prolonged series of antigovernment protests and strikes in 1998–99, after Norbert Zongo's assassination, the authorities tried to appease critics by agreeing to a series of political reforms and promising to build a monument to Sankara and the three other official national heroes (Ouezzin Coulibaly, Philippe Zinda Kaboré, and Nazi Boni). That Monument to the National Heroes was finally inaugurated in Ouagadougou in December 2010, during celebrations to mark the country's fiftieth anniversary of independence.

Sankara's grave also continued to serve as an informal monument, now encased in a concrete enclosure, whitewashed and adorned with the Burkinabè national colors.

Supporters and admirers of Sankara have held commemorative gatherings there each year. The one on October 15, 2007—the twentieth anniversary of his death—was especially large. Many thousands turned out, with unruly crowds growing so big that the organizers had difficulty controlling them. An emotional highpoint was the appearance of Mariam Sankara, the late president's widow, who had gone into exile with her two sons shortly after the coup. Returning to Burkina Faso for the first time since then, she laid flowers at her husband's gravesite. While some of the organizers had known Sankara personally, many in the crowd were too young to have had any direct memories of their own. "The ideal of Thomas Sankara is still here, through all these youth who are mobilized, all these people," his widow told a reporter.

Sankara's ideas were clearly starting to reach a new generation. Even the state-owned daily *Sidwaya* felt compelled to acknowledge that Sankara was viewed as a pan-African hero, within Burkina Faso and across the continent, in league with figures such as Marcus Garvey, Kwame Nkrumah, Malcolm X, Patrice Lumumba, Sékou Touré, and Cheick Anta Diop. "Twenty years after his death," the newspaper commented, "his pan-Africanist ideas remain intact in the memory of Africa's peoples, in particular its youth."

A demonstration of Sankara's external appeal came during the twentieth anniversary commemoration as well. Weeks before, an international "Thomas Sankara

Caravan" departed from Chiapas, Mexico. It was initiated by Odile Sankara, one of the late president's sisters, and a Chadian musician teaching in Mexico. The group of Africans and Mexicans then flew to France, and by land passed through Switzerland and Italy, addressing rallies of hundreds of people along the way and picking up more international participants. They then flew to Senegal and traveled by land through Mali, addressing yet more rallies, before finally arriving in Ouagadougou on the eve of the anniversary to a large welcoming crowd.

Whether at anniversary commemorations or on other occasions, it has not been uncommon to see young people across West Africa wearing Sankara T-shirts. Activists can readily find his words, whether from printed collections of his speeches and interviews (published in French as well as English editions) or on the website http://thomassankara.net. Hip-hop and reggae musicians from Mali, Senegal, and Burkina Faso have released popular songs and videos sampling passages from Sankara's speeches. In Senegal, the rapper-activists of "Y'en a marre," an opposition group with a fervent following among youths in poor neighborhoods, have gone to rallies sporting T-shirts with Sankara's portrait and the message, "I'm still here."

"Above all, Sankara's ongoing popularity is due to the ideas and values he embodied," Demba Moussa Dembèlè, director of the African Forum on Alternatives in Dakar, has written. "If Sankara arouses as much fervor today as he did more than two decades ago, it is because he embodied and defended causes that resonate today among the world's oppressed."

Selected Bibliography

Andriamirado, Sennen. *Il s'appelait Sankara.* Paris: Jeune
　　Afrique livres, 1989.

———. *Sankara le rebelle.* Paris: Jeune Afrique livres, 1987.

Bazié, Jean Hubert. *Chronique du Burkina.* Ouagadougou:
　　Imprimerie de la direction générale de la presse écrite,
　　1985.

Englebert, Pierre. *Burkina Faso: Unsteady Statehood in West
　　Africa.* Boulder, CO: Westview, 1996.

Harrison, Paul. *The Greening of Africa.* Harmondsworth:
　　Penguin, 1987.

Harsch, Ernest. "Burkina Faso: A Revolution Derailed."
　　Africa Report 33, no. 1 (January–February 1988): 33–39.

———. "The Legacies of Thomas Sankara: A Revolutionary
　　Experience in Retrospect." *Review of African Political
　　Economy* 40, no. 137 (September 2013): 358–74.

———. "Thomas Sankara (1949–1987)." In *Dictionary
　　of African Biography,* vol. 5, edited by Emmanuel K.
　　Akyeampong and Henry Louis Gates, Jr., 268–70.
　　Oxford: Oxford University Press, 2012.

Jaffré, Bruno. *Biographie de Thomas Sankara: La patrie ou la
　　mort . . . .* 2nd ed. Paris: L'Harmattan, 2007.

———. *Burkina Faso: Les Années Sankara, de la révolution à
　　la rectification.* Paris: L'Harmattan, 1989.

Otayek, René, Filiga Michel Sawadogo, and Jean-Pierre Guingané, eds. *Le Burkina entre révolution et démocratie (1983–1993)*. Paris: Karthala, 1996.

Prairie, Michel, ed. *Thomas Sankara Speaks: The Burkina Faso Revolution, 1983–87*. 2nd ed. New York: Pathfinder Press, 2007.

Sankara, Thomas, and François Mitterrand. "La joute verbale Sankara Mitterrand (texte intégral), 17 novembre 1986," http://thomassankara.net/spip.php?article32 (accessed October 23, 2012).

Sawadogo, Alfred Yambangba. *Le président Thomas Sankara. Chef de la révolution Burkinabè: 1983–1987. Portrait.* Paris: L'Harmattan, 2001.

Skinner, Elliot P. "Sankara and the Burkinabè Revolution: Charisma and Power, Local and External Dimensions." *Journal of Modern African Studies* 26, no. 3 (September 1988): 437–55.

Somé, Valère D. *Thomas Sankara: L'espoir assassiné.* Paris: L'Harmattan, 1990.

Ziegler, Jean, and Jean-Philippe Rapp. *Sankara: Un nouveau pouvoir africain.* Paris: Editions Pierre-Marcel Favre, 1986.

Interviews by Ernest Harsch

Basile Guissou. Ouagadougou, March 12, 1985.

Ernest Nongma Ouédraogo. Ouagadougou, March 4, 1999.

Youssouf Ouédraogo. Ouagadougou, March 15, 1985.

Paul Sankara. Washington, DC, May 30, 2013.

Thomas Sankara. New York, October 2, 1984, and Ouagadougou, March 17, 1985.

Ahmadu Toumani Touré. New York, September 26, 1996.

Website

http://thomassankara.net

Videos

Association Baraka. *Sur les traces de Thomas Sankara . . . Héritage en partages.* Baraka Studios, 2008, 180 minutes.

Balufu, Bakupa-Kanyinda. *Thomas Sankara.* Paris: Myriapodus Films, 1991, 26 minutes.

Ho, Thuy Tien. *Burkina Faso, un révolution rectifiée.* Paris: Solferino Images, 2011, 52 minutes.

Shuffield, Robin. *Thomas Sankara: The Upright Man.* Amazon/CreateSpace, 2009, 53 minutes.

Index

Afghanistan, 116
African Independence Party. *See* PAI
African Union. *See* OAU
agrarian reform, 97–98
agriculture, 89–90, 94–97
Algeria, 117
Alpha Commando, 77, 83
ANC (African National Congress), 118–19
anticorruption, 61–63, 139–42; asset disclosures, 104–5, 140–42
armed forces reforms, 64–67, 81

Bambata Forum, 119–20
Barro, Justin Damo, 92
Battle of the Rail, 76
Benin, 124
Bishop, Maurice, 46
Bobo, 21, 85
Boni, Nazi, 150
Botha, Pik, 108
Burkina Faso, 84; ethnic groups, 84–85; languages, 84–86; name change, 56, 85; poverty, 34–35, 148; religions, 84; territorial divisions, 69–70. *See also* Upper Volta

Burkinabè Communist Group. *See* GBC

Canada, 115
Carrefour africain, 40, 74
Castro, Fidel, 46, 116
CDRs (Committees for the Defense of the Revolution), 53, 66–69, 78, 81–83, 97–98, 104; abuses by, 102, 132–35
Chad, 110
chiefs, traditional, 68–69, 98, 143
China, 115
CMRPN (Military Committee for the Enhancement of National Progress), 38–43
CNR (National Council of the Revolution), 51–54, 72, 90, 110–11; differences within, 128–31, 137–39, 144, 147
Committees for the Defense of the Revolution. *See* CDRs
Comoros, 110
Compaoré, Blaise, 35, 39, 44, 49–50, 53, 126, 128–29, 135, 140–42; coup (1987), 127–30, 143–47, 149; post-coup practices, 147–48
Côte d'Ivoire, 22, 84, 124–26, 130, 148

Coulibaly, Ouezzin, 23, 150
Council for the Welfare of the People. *See* CSP
CPPC (People's Commission for the Prevention of Corruption), 140–42
CSP (Council for the Welfare of the People), 43–51
Cuba, 46, 116–
culture, 86–87

daba (hoe), 95
Dagnoën cemetery, 128, 148
decentralization, 67–70
Dembélé, Demba Moussa, 152
democracy, 17, 55
Diendéré, Gilbert, 145, 148
Diop, Cheick Anta, 151
Directorate for Women's Mobilization and Organization, 82
Dumont, René, 28

economic policy, 88, 90–93; aid, 91–93; austerity, 63, 93–94; foreign debt, 121–22; private sector, 105–6; state enterprises, 103–5; taxation, 93–94, 105
education, 72, 77, 83–84, 94
elders, 74–75
El Salvador, 46
environment, 98–103; "three struggles," 101–2; tree planting, 100, 102–3

Faso dan Fani, 106–7
Foccart, Jacques, 130
France, 21–23, 48–49, 92, 108–2, 121, 125, 130, 148; as colonial authority, 15, 21–22, 84

Francophonie, La, 111–112
French language, 13, 51, 85–86, 111–12
Fulfuldé, 13, 85–87

Garvey, Marcus, 151
GBC (Burkinabè Communist Group), 137
Ghana, 122–24
Gourmantché, 21
Gourounsi, 21, 51, 85
government, 53, 64, 80
Grenada, 46, 115
Guébré, Fidèle, 51
Guissou, Basile, 91

Harlem, 113–14
Harrison, Paul, 78
Haute-Volta. *See* Upper Volta
health, 77–78, 94
Houphouët-Boigny, Félix, 125–26, 130, 142

IMF (International Monetary Fund), 92, 94
Israel, 115

Jaffré, Bruno, 30
Japan, 115
Johnson, Prince, 130
Jula, 13, 85–87

Kaboré, Boukary, 147
Kaboré, Philippe Zinda, 150
Kafando, Hyacinthe, 145
Kiemdé, Frédéric, 129, 135
Kilimité, Hien, 44
Ki-Zerbo, Joseph, 134

labor mobilizations, 71–76
Lamizana, Sangoulé, 24, 32–33, 37–38, 62

League for Patriotic Development. *See* Lipad
Liberia, 130
Libya, 46, 116–17
Lingani, Jean-Baptiste, 44, 47–50, 53, 129, 149
Lipad (League for Patriotic Development), 137–38
literacy campaign, 77, 83–84, 86
Lobi, 21
Lumumba, Patrice, 151

Machel, Samora, 46
Madagascar, 27–29
Malcolm X, 151
Mali, 18, 84, 124–25, 130, 152; wars with Burkina Faso, 31–32, 66–67, 124–25, 132
Mandela, Nelson, 108, 118
Mauritania, 119
Military Committee for the Enhancement of National Progress. *See* CMRPN
Mitterrand, François, 15, 17, 48, 108, 110, 112
mogho naba (Mossi emperor), 21
Mooré, 13, 51, 85–87
Morocco, 119, 121
Mossi, 20–21, 84–87, 142–
Mozambique, 46

"naam" peasants' movement, 75
Namibia, 117–120
National Council of the Revolution. *See* CNR
Netherlands, 115
New Caledonia, 111
Newsweek, 88, 92–93
Nicaragua, 15, 46, 115–17
Niger, 84, 124
Nkrumah, Kwame, 151

Non-Aligned Movement, 46, 116

OAU (Organization of African Unity), 107, 117–19, 121–22
Observateur, L', 40, 45, 132
OMR (Revolutionary Military Organization), 137, 144, 147
Ortega, Daniel, 116
Ouédraogo, Ernest Nongma, 41, 59, 61, 141–
Ouédraogo, Jean-Baptiste, 44–45, 48–50
Ouédraogo, Youssouf, 74, 91–92

PAI (African Independence Party), 26, 35, 135, 137–38
Palestine, 15, 115
pan-Africanism, 110, 117, 119, 151
Penne, Guy, 48–49
People's Commission for the Prevention of Corruption. *See* CPPC
People's Development Program. *See* PPD
People's Revolutionary Tribunals. *See* TPRs
Peulh, 20–21, 85
Pô, 32–35, 39, 48–50, 123
Polisario Front, 121
Popular Front, 128, 147
PPD (People's Development Program), 73–74, 100–101

al-Qaddafi, Muammar, 46

Rawlings, Jerry John, 122–24
Ratsiraka, Didier, 28–29
Reagan, Ronald, 113
repression, 41–42, 131–36, 148–49

Revolutionary Military Organization. *See* OMR

SADR (Sahrawi Arab Democratic Republic), 121
Samo, 21
Sankara, Auguste, 44
Sankara, Joseph, 20–21
Sankara, Marguerite (née Kinda), 20
Sankara, Mariam (née Serme), 34, 58, 151
Sankara, Odile, 152
Sankara, Paul, 29, 58–59
Sankara, Pauline, 29
Sankara, Philippe, 34
Sankara, Thomas
    childhood, 20–24
    family, 20–23, 29, 34, 58–59
    military training, 24–29
    army commands, 29–34, 39
    in Mali war (1974), 31–32
    as minister of information, 39–42
    as prime minister, 45–48
    arrest (1983), 48–49
    August 4, 1983, takeover, 50–53
    and CNR, 53–54
    ideology, 15, 47, 52–55
    leadership style, 14, 40, 56–61
    assets, 140–41
    death, 19, 127–28, 144–45
    legacy, 149–53
Sankarists, 149–50
Sawadogo, Alfred, 59–60, 102
Senegal, 26, 152
Sidwaya, 103, 151
Silmi-Mossi, 20, 85
Somé, Valère, 48, 53, 135, 137, 143–44, 147

Somé Yorian, Gabriel, 43–44, 49–51
South Africa, 17, 108, 114, 117–20
Soviet Union, 115–17, 139
SWAPO (South West Africa People's Organization), 118–19

Tarnue, John, 130
Terrasson de Fougères, Chantal (Compaoré), 126, 141–42
Tiendrébéogo, Didier, 132
Toé, Fidèle, 23, 40, 140
Togo, 124, 130, 148
Touré, Adama, 26–27
Touré, Ahmadou Toumani, 18
Touré, Sékou, 151
Touré, Soumane, 23, 41, 135, 138
TPRs (People's Revolutionary Tribunals), 61–63, 65, 86, 104, 133, 139–40
Traoré, Aïcha, 81
Traoré, Alouna, 144–45
Traoré, Moussa, 18
Tuareg, 21

UCB (Union of Burkinabè Communists), 135, 137–38
UFB (Women's Union of Burkina), 13, 83–84
ULC (Union of Communist Struggle), 137
ULCR (Union of Communist Struggle-Reconstructed), 137–38, 147
UNICEF, 77–78
Union of Burkinabè Communists. *See* UCB
Union of Communist Struggle. *See* ULC

Union of Communist Struggle-Reconstructed. *See* ULCR
unions, 41, 45, 134–36
United Nations address, 110, 114–15
United States, 17, 92–93, 113–15
Upper Volta, 15, 21–22, 31, 84. *See also* Burkina Faso

Vaccination Commando, 77–78
Vietnam, 112

water, 89, 96, 100–101
Western Sahara, 119, 121

women, 13–14, 79–84, 106–7
Women's Union of Burkina. *See* UFB
World Bank, 76, 92, 94

Yaméogo, Maurice, 23–24, 44
"Y'en a marre," 152
Young, Andrew, 113
youth, 74–75

Zerbo, Saye, 38–39, 42–43, 62, 134
Zongo, Henri, 42, 44, 48–50, 53, 111, 129, 149
Zongo, Norbert, 148, 150